Short Thoughts for the Long Haul

Robert Brault

<>‹›‹>

Books by Robert Brault

Round Up The Usual Subjects

The Second Collection

Reflections

Short Thoughts for the Long Haul

<>‹>‹>

For Joan

"He was a sad and lonesome clown,
And she was the circus that came to town."

<>‹>‹>

Short Thoughts for the Long Haul (C) 2017 by Robert Brault

The author welcomes reader comments at his website, ***rbrault.blogspot.com*** and email address, ***bobbrault@att.net***.

Created and published using the Amazon CreateSpace Independent Publishing Platform.

ISBN-13: 978-1548472818
ISBN-10: 1548472816

Front Cover: "Fishing at Dusk" ~~ pastel by Joan Brault

<>＜>＜>

Author's Note

I want to underscore the fact that all writings in this book are original.

Some may ring familiar, having appeared on the internet and in media outlets around the world. I've been pleased to see my thoughts quoted on more than a million internet sites since 2009 and today one or another of my items is quoted on Twitter about every ten minutes.

It is difficult to protect one's creative rights to short writings such as these, and I am accustomed to seeing my items credited to others, often to the famous. This book is a hopeful attempt to lay claim to the major part of my work. That said, I do encourage the free, non-commercial use of my items, asking only attribution. I expect commercial users to contact me for permission.

Robert Brault
bobbrault@att.net

<>< ><>

Table of Topics

<>< ><>

<><><>

~~~

Enjoy the little things, for one day you may look back and realize they were the big things.

~~~

<>‹>‹>

Preface

My goal in this volume is to bring together the "best" of my internet thoughts in one anthology collection. For the most part, I have left the judgment of "best" to my internet readers, deferring to their "likes" and "retweets" and direct comments as the measure. I have only here and there acceded to my own questionable judgment in the matter.

The book's contents are drawn mainly from my previous three books, *Round Up The Usual Subjects, The Second Collection* and *Reflections,* all of which were partial collections of my internet work. Interspersed are the more popular of my newer online postings.

To characterize the writings, and to provide a little background to my own unlikely history as a writer, I present once again the preface to my first book, *Round Up The Usual Subjects.* It remains, I think, an apt introduction.

~~~

"In 1961, while in college, I sold a Picturesque Speech item to Reader's Digest. So began an avocation that has extended to this day. For the next thirty years, I programmed computers for a living and wrote aphorisms for pleasure. Some 1200 made their way into magazines and newspapers between 1961 and 1994.

<><><>

In 2009, seven years into retirement, and after a 15-year recess from writing, I launched an internet blog called *A Robert Brault Reader*. My hope was to find a new audience for my published writings. To my surprise, the effort reawakened the old muse, and new thoughts began to flow.

The blog was noticed by Terri Guillemets at The Quote Garden, the internet's most frequented quote site. She soon was showcasing some 400 of my items, each with a hyperlink back to my site. Soon thereafter, a Google search would routinely turn up a million sites quoting my items. Today, although I blog only occasionally, I find myself quoted on Twitter several hundreds times a day.

This book is a selection of quotes originating in the blog or on Twitter, interspersed here and there with a bit of verse. The quotes are arranged by topic, the topics in alphabetical order. My hope is that the book will serve as both a quick reference and an entertaining bedside browse.

I have indeed selected the quotes with an eye toward entertainment. You will find little preaching here and no political commentary, save a few potshots at the foibles of politicians generally. There is no religious advocacy, although my thoughts are strongly sympathetic to those who find a need for God in their lives.

<><><>

*The thoughts, for the most part, are geared to
tried and true virtues -- to faith, hope and charity,
to pluck and optimism, to tolerance, compassion
and understanding. Mixed in, you will find a
healthy dollop of the wry, the sly and the facetious,
but you will find no malice.*

*Will you find wisdom in these pages? Yes, but
only the wisdom you bring to them. My goal is to
put into words that which we all know full well but
seldom express. The deal, as I tell my blog readers,
is that I supply the words, you supply the insight."*

~~~

That said, I do hope you enjoy the book.

Robert Brault
June 2017

<><><>

~~~

There is nothing instructive in a wise saying. It does not impart to you a skill; it does not provide you new information. It is education in the purest sense -- a drawing out of what has been latent in your understanding. Your pleasure in the saying does not come from having learned something new but from having something you knew elucidated and confirmed. What we call wisdom is the awakening of the mind to what we already know in our hearts.

~~~

Achievement

Keynote Thought

A nod,
A bow
and a tip of the lid
to the person
who coulda
and shoulda
and did!

Observations

There is no limit to what one person can do, and,
fortunately, that is who most of us are.

~~~

Before you recite the reasons why you can't, try to
imagine them as the reasons why you didn't.

~~~

There is no such thing as a list of reasons. There is either
one sufficient reason or a list of excuses.

~~~

Achievement

Everything happens for the purpose of what you decide to do about it.

~~~

To achieve success, you can't let failure stop you. To achieve great success, you can't let success stop you.

~~~

Right now, before you do it, is the time to ask what you might have done differently.

~~~

The most common obstacle to achievement is a schedule already full.

~~~

Life is too short to wait for an answer, especially when the answer is nearly always, "It's up to you."

~~~

The trouble with leaving yourself a way out is that you always take it.

~~~

More important sometimes than perseverance is the knack of avoiding obstacles that are not in your way.

~~~

There is always a good excuse, always a reason not to. The hardest freedom to win is the freedom from our excuses.

~~~

The danger in life is that we will choose to go nowhere because we know the way... choose to do nothing because we know how.

~~~

No one pays us for our time and effort. We are paid to produce something, and it's important to remind ourselves each day what it is.

~~~

A watershed moment in life is the day you realize that what you can or can't do is a decision, not a recollection.

~~~

The enemy of great dreams is not so much the cynic as the small dreamer.

~~~

Though the barriers of life seem formidable, we find when we challenge them that they have no will to resist.

~~~

Achievement

If You Want My Advice

Never be discouraged by the opinion of people who don't know what you're about to accomplish.

~~~

No matter what you hear said about yourself, do what you would do if you hadn't heard it.

~~~

Always list things to do in doable order.

~~~

Never act until you have clearly answered the question, "What happens if I do nothing?"

~~~

Never let probability stop you. It is, and always has been, a notorious liar.

~~~

Show up, work hard, learn from your mistakes, and in the end it will all seem like a strategy.

~~~

The Voice of Experience

If your only goal is to achieve security, there are two things you will never achieve: (1) security; (2) anything else.

~~~

You can waste a lot of time debating whether the only way is the easiest way.

~~~

The most basic strategy is to get time on your side. The most basic tactic is to sit and wait.

~~~

When everything worth doing has been done, there will be plenty worth undoing.

A Reminder

If you haven't time to respond to a tug at your pants leg, your schedule is too crowded.

~~~

Adversity

Keynote Thought

Usually when the obstacles in your path cannot be overcome, it's not your path.

Observations

So often what seems like an impossible climb is just a staircase without the steps drawn in.

~~~

Sometimes you feel like giving up, but then you look at other people who have given up, and the results aren't that good.

~~~

A river never beats its head against obstacles. It always go around, and it always gets to the sea.

~~~

Where the loser saw barriers, the winner saw hurdles.

~~~

When life takes the wind out of your sails, it is to test you at the oars.

~~~

The thing to remember, when everyone seems to doubt you, is that everyone has not been born yet.

Speaking For Myself

The last time I failed, it made me double my effort, and it worked so well that I'm thinking of failing again.

Dry, Sly and Wry

Never mind the odds against you. If you double your effort, what will the odds against you do -- send for reinforcements?

~~~

Some days are such perfect disasters that there's nothing to do but sit back and admire their perfection.

~~~

Often it's just a short swim from the shipwreck of your life to the island paradise of your dreams, assuming you don't drown in the metaphor.

~~~

<><><>

Aging

Keynote Thought

*Two things you discover when you're older and wiser --
you're not actually any wiser, and behind the wrinkles,
you're not any older, either.*

Observations

*You're never too old, but you're always too young to
know it.*

~~~

*It is possible at any age to discover a lifelong desire you
never knew you had.*

~~~

*There is a time in life when you not only have
bittersweet memories but you make bittersweet plans.*

~~~

*Say what you want about aging, it's still the only way
to have old friends.*

~~~

Father Time keeps pitching the years at us. We swing and miss at a few. We hit a few out of the park. We try not to take any called strikes.

~~~

You find in old age that it is possible to revisit the past, the only requirement being that you come as you are.

~~~

Eventually you realize that your whole life has been preparation, and you begin to wonder if the rest might be preparation, too.

~~~

Who does not wish to be beautiful and clever and rich and to have back in old age the time spent trying to be any of them?

~~~

It is never too late, especially when it would otherwise be too late.

~~~

My advice? Never use the passing years as an excuse for old age.

~~~

<><><>

Aging

*You get to an age when no matter what happens, you
wish someone would put a stop to it.*

~~~

*If you wonder why older couples do not more often hug
and kiss, you do not appreciate the intimacy of just
growing old together.*

~~~

*You complain of the passing years, but then you look in
a mirror and realize that very few of them actually got
past.*

~~~

*You spend the first two-thirds of your life asking to be
left alone and the last third not having to ask.*

~~~

*What you notice as the years go by is that your friends
keep getting older while strangers keep getting younger.*

~~~

*The older you get, the more time you like to spend with
people who are glad to see you.*

~~~

Speaking For Myself

In this, the late afternoon of my life, I wonder, "Am I casting a longer shadow, or is my shadow casting a shorter me?"

~~~

Having nearly completed the book of life, I can tell you that the answers are not in the back.

Reflections

An old woman looks in a mirror, recalls a little girl with a rag doll, and wonders what became of the little girl.

~~~

*The mind, as you age,
Is an artist, it seems.
Monet paints your mem'ries,
Picasso your dreams.*

~~~

Animals

Keynote Thought

Man is rated the highest animal, at least among the animals who returned the questionnaire.

Observations

The only animal whose natural habitat is a zoo is the zookeeper.

~~~

There is in every animal a sense of duty that man condescends to call instinct.

~~~

It is a perverse human perception that animals in their native habitat are running wild.

~~~

The smarter the animal, the more adept it is at pretending to be trained.

~~~

<>< ><>

Animals

The great thing about advocating for animals is that it's so easy to please your base constituency.

~~~

Man is the only trained animal who expects his reward before he does his trick.

~~~

For the most part we carnivores do not eat other carnivores. We prefer to eat our vegetarian friends.

~~~

If animals could talk, the world would lose its best listeners.

~~~

If man were freed of all superstition and all prejudice, and had replaced these with a keen sensitivity to his real environment, and moreover had developed a means of communication so simplified that a single syllable could express his every desire, then he would have achieved the level of intelligence already achieved by his dog.

~~~

<><><>

Animals

Speaking For Myself

I believe in animal rights, and high among them is the right to the gentle stroke of a human hand.

~~~

There are times when I need the company of people, and times when I need the company of creatures who were never expelled from paradise for wanting to become God.

Dry, Sly and Wry

If a rabbit defined intelligence the way man does, then the most intelligent animal would be a rabbit, followed by the animal most willing to obey the commands of a rabbit.

~~~

Man is the only animal who enjoys the consolation of believing in a next life. All other animals enjoy the consolation of not worrying about it.

~~~

Evidence suggests that every life form on earth was given a choice of intelligence or perfection, and all but one chose perfection.

~~~

<><><>

Apology

Keynote Thought

Life becomes easier when you learn to accept an apology you never got.

Observations

An important thing to get to know about a person is the unspoken ways they say they're sorry.

~~~

You don't always have to be the one at fault to be the one who's sorry.

~~~

We deny an apology to the person we owe it to, and then one day they are gone, and we apologize to anyone who will listen.

~~~

An apology is that rare obligation that has no due date. If it is owed, it is due.

~~~

<><><>

Apology

Too often an apology is a letter written but never mailed.

Speaking For Myself

If I had it to do over, there'd be a hand I'd take and a silence I'd break.

~~~

I've learned this about apologizing, "I'm sorry <u>that</u>" is a better start than "I'm sorry <u>if</u>."

~~~

Just once, when someone says, "I'm sorry if you took offense," I'd like to reply, "Come back when you're sorry you gave it."

~~~

If You Want My Advice

It is always a good idea to ask the Lord's forgiveness, but do not confuse it with having apologized.

~~~

<> <> <>

Art & Artists

*Whatever the art form, it is about capturing a moment
and storing it out of the reach of time.*

Observations

*Art is an innate distrust of the theory of reality
concocted by the five senses.*

~~~

*The artist uses the talent he has, wishing he had more
talent. The talent uses the artist it has, wishing it had
more artist.*

~~~

*To the artist, Genesis is a tale of six days in which the
Creator suggested some really good ideas.*

~~~

It is easier to reach perfection than to stop there.

~~~

There is in art the notion that less is more, which is to say, you don't torture a painting that has already confessed.

~~~

The painter needs all the talent of the poet, plus hand-eye coordination.

~~~

That portion of reality that can be composed within a frame can be understood.

~~~

What you often see in a lesser work of art is a subject perfectly captured but never set free.

~~~

Ah, but a man's reach should exceed his grasp, said Browning, and so it has, extended by the length of pen and brush.

~~~

Dry, Sly and Wry

The artist wonders, "Have I barely scratched the surface of my talent, or is scratching a surface all the talent I have?"

~~~

An artist must marry his talent -- and the two must elope. A big church wedding is fatal.

~~~

A painting is what you make of it, besides which, "Moon Weeping" has a better ring to it than, "Paintbrush Dripping."

~~~

The first assumption of an art critic is that the artist meant to paint something else.

~~~

The poet puts pen to paper. The painter puts brush to canvas. The poet has the easier task, for his pen does not alter his rhyme.

~~~

<><><>

Oh, how much simpler
Things would be
If eyes could paint
Or brush could see.

You Be The Quotesmith

There is in every artist's studio a scrapheap of
discarded works in which the artist's _____
prevailed against his _____.

Selections

hand
eye
brush
imagination
daring
discipline
talent
[other]

Example:
There is in every artist's studio a scrapheap of
discarded works in which the artist's <u>discipline</u>
prevailed against his <u>daring</u>.

~~~

<><><>

Attitude

Keynote Thought

There are exactly as many special occasions in life as we choose to celebrate.

Observations

Nothing in life means a thing unless somebody cares, and the whole trick is to keep being that somebody.

~~~

If you can be unaccountably sad, you can be unaccountably happy.

~~~

Two people can have a middling day, but one rounds up and the other rounds down.

~~~

Things happen to justify whatever mood you're in.

~~~

<><><>

Attitude

One thing you notice about the strangers you meet on
the street is that they tend to be having the same sort
of day you are.

~~~

You can allow yourself to feel offended, belittled,
snubbed -- there's always cause for it. There just isn't
time for it.

~~~

You begin to find what you're looking for in life when
you begin to look for what you're finding.

~~~

If you could trade lives with a happy person, he or she
would be just as happy with yours.

~~~

If You Want My Advice

The way to dispel negative thoughts is to insist that
they have a purpose.

~~~

As a jobseeker, remember this -- you only lack experience if they want it done the same old way.

~~~

Before you call any work menial, watch a proud person do it.

~~~

Refuse to be burdened by vague worries. If something wants to worry you, insist that it make itself clear.

Speaking For Myself

We find things where we look for them, which is why I never look for a golf ball out of bounds.

~~~

I have no idea what heaven is like, but I know people who will enjoy it and I know people who won't.

~~~

<>

Be Yourself

If God had wanted a better you, He would have created a better you, and that's the challenge -- He did.

Observations

We all have our limitations, but when we listen to our critics, we also have theirs.

~~~

Of what use to get what you want in life if you must become someone else to get it?

~~~

*Present yourself always
As who you would be,
And that is the person
The world will see.*

~~~

There is a limit to how much you can change to be liked for who you really are.

~~~

You can be the person it takes to get what you want, or you can be the person you want and take what you get.

~~~

What you discover about people you try not to offend is that you can offend them without trying.

~~~

Looking back, you realize that a very special person passed briefly through your life. That person was you. It is not too late to become that person again.

~~~

It is important to be your own friend, especially on days when you wouldn't care to make your own acquaintance.

~~~

Why try to be someone you're not? Life is hard enough without adding impersonation to the skills required.

~~~

Be Yourself

If you can't figure out who you are, you might as well work on who you want to be.

~~~

You can try to be someone else, but it's easier to just be yourself and apologize as necessary.

~~~

If you let the world treat you like a nobody, you have nobody to blame.

~~~

If You Want My Advice

Never mind searching for who you are. Search for the person you aspire to be.

~~~

Do what you must,
And your friends will adjust.

~~~

Be always demanding of the person you are -- and forgiving of the person you were.

~~~

Always laugh off a slight insult, so that people will know what it means when you're not laughing.

~~~

Do not look to find your identity in some particular work. Look to stamp your identity on whatever work you do.

~~~

Never mind what the world expects of you. It is too low a standard to be concerned about.

~~~

Know thyself, for it greatly lessens the danger that you will accidentally reveal it to someone else.

~~~

Know thyself, especially thyself after a couple of drinks.

~~~

There are always people who think they have you all figured out. Treasure them. They are your advantage in life.

~~~

Dry, Sly and Wry

It's annoying to be disapproved of by people who know only half the story, especially when you're not sure which half they know.

~~~

All your life you pretend to be someone else, and it turns out you were someone else pretending to be you.

~~~

Ever wonder why people think you should know better when you've never given them any reason to think so?

~~~

The most important thing to know about yourself is where you usually leave your car keys.

~~~

So it turns out that all those years they were calling you a dim bulb, they meant you were efficient.

~~~

There's nothing like an old photo of yourself to remind you how many people have hid out behind that same face.

~~~

Eventually people come to understand you, and you wonder why you ever thought that would improve things.

~~~

Sometimes you just wish you could be someone else, although not usually anyone you've actually met.

Speaking For Myself

Long ago I discovered the real me. The meeting was cordial, the decision to part mutual, and we remain friends.

~~~

If God had intended me to make excuses for who I am, He would have given me better excuses.

~~~

Yes, I've been accused of wasting my time, to which I reply, "Whose time did you say that was again?"

~~~

<><><>

Be Yourself

I am told to just be myself, but as much as I have practiced the impression, I am still no good at it.

~~~

The reason it's so difficult to discover who we really are is that we tend to be looking for a more talented version.

~~~

Every day I go forth to seek my identity, feeling greatly blessed by the things I don't find it in.

~~~

Truth is, I am still searching for myself -- and grateful to anyone who can tell me where I was last seen.

~~~

Perhaps if people really knew me, they would understand me, but I'd rather be misunderstood than really known.

~~~

It is possible, I think, to become the person you were born to be and decide you can do better.

~~~

<>\<><\>

Beauty

Keynote Thought

To be loved is to beautiful in someone's eyes, and when you think about it, is there any other way to be beautiful?

Observations

We ask, "What do they see in each other?" when the question should be, "What do they choose to overlook?"

~~~

The secret to feeling beautiful is to find someone who thinks you are and let them convince you.

~~~

Inner beauty, too, needs occasionally to be told it is beautiful.

~~~

It is a rare woman who can overcome her desire to remain pretty and allow herself to become beautiful.

~~~

<><><>

Beauty

We try to preserve our good looks by covering up all traces of age and end up revealing our age by covering up all traces of good looks.

~~~

There is no actual law that says a person of inner beauty cannot also maintain an appearance.

~~~

Dry, Sly and Wry

No one ever chose to become a scintillating conversationalist who had the option of just standing there, looking great.

~~~

Ever wonder how a hotel bathroom mirror knows what you will look like in twenty years?

~~~

Eventually you realize that you have pretty much the face your mom warned you might freeze that way if you weren't careful.

~~~

Belief

Keynote Thought

Sometimes you believe a thing that isn't true, because in the world you wish to live in, it would be true.

~~~

Observations

To believe only what you know to be true is to seriously underappreciate the possibilities of belief.

~~~

An old belief is like an old shoe -- we so value its comfort that we fail to notice the hole in it.

~~~

The difference between truth and belief is that belief is not always on your side.

~~~

It is hard to challenge a belief that people do not insist be true.

~~~

<><><>

Belief

It is one thing to have made up your mind and another thing to have made up your eyes and ears.

~~~

There is no belief so preposterous that something more preposterous cannot be cited as further proof.

~~~

When we sacrifice truth to some self-serving belief, we tend to believe it tenaciously, for it has come at such great sacrifice.

~~~

Anyone can believe on the evidence. It takes an inquisitive mind to believe on a strange, unaccountable lack of evidence.

~~~

Nostalgia is largely the memory of things we once believed.

~~~

Sometimes there are words you'd be ready to believe again, if only someone would say them again.

~~~

Speaking For Myself

A rule I try to follow is this: Never believe anything that requires you to hate people who do not believe it.

~~~

You can hold beliefs that give you an advantage in life, but, please, don't go around calling them principles.

~~~

In one compartment of my brain reside my doubts. In the compartment directly below reside my beliefs -- and my beliefs keep pounding on the ceiling and shouting, "Be quiet up there!"

~~~

If You Want My Advice

Beware a belief that has long withstood the test of not being challenged.

~~~

<><><>

Charity

Keynote Thought

The willingness to share does not make one charitable; it makes one free.

Observations

Eventually you realize that nothing that benefits you and you alone benefits anyone.

~~~

So often the answer to our prayers is to become the answer to someone else's prayers.

~~~

There's a lot selfishness that goes by the name of minding your own business.

~~~

Act always from a sense of common humanity, and let others decide if it be charity.

~~~

<><><>

It is an act of charity to coax someone down from a ledge, for nearly always we are reaching out from our own ledge.

If You Want My Advice

Never say to someone in need, "You know where to reach me." Observe, instead, that they have already reached you.

Words Of My Mother

"Helping someone in need is not charity; it is proper etiquette."

"Delay never made a kindness any kinder."

Words From a Diary

"Today I bent the truth to be kind, and I have no regret, for I am far surer of what is kind than I am of what is true."

~~~

<>‹›‹›

Childhood

Keynote Thought

If you can recall what the world was like when you were a wide-eyed kid, then you know what the world is like right now.

Observations

To trade a childhood wonder for a plausible explanation -- is there a worse trade we make in life?

~~~

The thing most missed from childhood days is the ability to recognize happiness while in progress.

~~~

In the happiest of our childhood memories, our parents were happy, too.

~~~

We do not recognize how fragile a thing childhood is until it becomes our turn to create it for our kids.

~~~

For every childhood question, there is a preposterous answer that you weren't actually supposed to believe forever.

~~~

In childhood we press our nose to the pane, looking out. In memories of childhood, we press our nose to the pane, looking in.

~~~

The Fiction Of Childhood

It is not just the fiction of Santa Claus -- or the Easter Bunny or the Tooth Fairy -- we create for our kids but the fiction of childhood itself. It extends to summer evenings chasing fireflies and picnics by the lake, a make-believe world made possible by the illusion that Dad and Mom are in charge and there is nothing to fear.

~~~

Choice

Keynote Thought

We do not awaken each day to an array of choices. We awaken to a clear duty born of the choices we have made. And to what have we sacrificed our freedom? To the life we wish to live and to the people we wish to live it with.

Observations

We have a choice every day -- to act on yesterday's good intentions or get an early start on tomorrow's regrets.

~~~

So often we choose to continue the life we know, only to discover that it was not one of the choices.

~~~

You can awaken each day to obligations you never chose, or you can decide today to choose them.

~~~

<><><>

Civility

Keynote Thought

We undervalue the courage of common civility, for what do we know of another person's day, of their worries and anxieties, of how deep into their innermost resources they had to reach for that gracious smile, that pleasant hello.

Observations

How small a nod it would take, how fleeting a smile, to give someone you meet today a sense of self worth.

~~~

If today you can't be anything else to anyone, you can be the passing stranger who nodded hello.

~~~

A nod, a smile, a pleasant hello -- they aren't anything. And that's the point, a little civility doesn't take anything.

~~~

<><><>

Civility

There is no effect more disproportionate to its cause than the happiness bestowed by a small compliment.

~~~

The most basic civility is to accept people for what they pretend to be, even when they pretend badly.

~~~

You can be sure that the person who disparages others in your presence disparages you in their presence.

If You Want My Advice

Count no day lost in which you waited your turn, took only your share and sought advantage over no one.

~~~

Speaking For Myself

I am a guest in your life. You are a guest in mine. Not something calling for a dress code, maybe, but a little etiquette?

~~~

<>◇<>

Commitment

Keynote Thought

They who lack the energy for commitment greatly underestimate commitment as a source of energy.

~~~

Observations

Of what use is freedom of choice if you always choose freedom and never choose choice?

~~~

To commit to our choices is not to lose our freedom but to exercise it.

~~~

You have to decide what your duty is, or else others will decide for you, and they will all be experts on the subject.

~~~

A question to occasionally ask yourself: What did I approve today by remaining silent?

~~~

We usually recognize the consequence of our actions. It is the consequence of our inaction that gets confused with fate.

~~~

Not everything we do each day is from love or a promise made, but that is the place to start.

~~~

It is a rare couple that doesn't celebrate the anniversary of more than one promise.

~~~

So you're born, you die, and in between you try not to get involved. Good luck with that.

Words, Looking Back

Though battered by daring,
not sorry I dared.
Though sorrowed by caring,
not sorry I cared.

~~~

Compromise

Keynote Thought

Only among principled parties can there be compromise, and, of necessity, it must appear to be a compromise of principle. In fact, it is a discovery of principle, accomplished by leaving on the table prejudices and self-interests that only posed as principles. In the end, each party leaves the table more truly principled for the compromise.

~~~

<><><>

Cosmic Understanding

Keynote Thought

I would rather be me and have to explain the universe than be the universe and have to explain me.

~~~

Observations

In man's study of the cosmos, there has never been a mystery that a larger mystery would not explain.

~~~

The thing missing in man's quest to understand the universe is someone else's point of view.

~~~

Although science has found many pieces to the universal jigsaw puzzle, it has yet to find a side piece.

~~~

When you've failed all your life to solve a mystery, you must consider the chance that it is not a mystery.

~~~

Grist For The Thought Mill

One day, there will be only one thing left to understand, and when we come to understand it, it will change our understanding of everything else.

~~~

Inevitably the world will end, and everything human beings have done will fade into oblivion, and the one consolation is that it probably has happened before.

~~~

Science, too, has its faith in a mystical, unseen Holy Trinity, for what else is dark matter, dark flow and dark energy?

Speaking For Myself

My quest for cosmic understanding is a book I have picked up and put down many times, each time forgetting to insert a bookmark.

~~~

It's my luck that every time I feel I comprehend God's plan, I don't have a pencil with me.

~~~

I've always thought that the vastness of the night sky is an incredible example of what can be done with mirrors, assuming that's the way it was done.

~~~

In comparing religious belief to science, I try to remember that science is belief, also.

~~~

All it takes is one person who cares, and suddenly it is no longer a vast, uncaring universe.

Dry, Sly and Wry

What we know about the universe is that it began as a swirling pool of hot gas that, as it cooled, spun off the Ten Commandments.

~~~

The Night Sky

A trillion asterisks and no explanations.

~~~

<>< ><>

The Daily Grind

Keynote Thought

It's not just you. No one gets up in the morning and is entirely happy with the decision.

Observations

It's hard sometimes to remember that you woke up just a few hours ago with no intention whatever of antagonizing anyone.

~~~

In everyday life, one thing leads to another, and usually just when you think it already has.

~~~

There can be heroism in the moment, but courage is always in the day-to-day.

~~~

<><><>

The Daily Grind

Now and then it's good to list all the things you regularly do for which there was once a good reason.

~~~

What you discover about life's shell game is that it's hardest to follow the pea when you're the pea.

~~~

There is no actual law that says you can't get locked into a daily routine that makes you happy.

~~~

There is a reason you were born -- and a bunch of things you've got to do today regardless.

~~~

There is no daily chore so trivial that it cannot be made important by skipping it two days running.

~~~

A question to ask each morning is what you would do if you had the coming day to live over again.

~~~

If You Want My Advice

Never let anything ruin your day that is not on your list of things you will let ruin your day.

~~~

Whatever you're trying to prove, it's good to occasionally spend a day not trying to prove it.

The Daily Commute

A commuter tie-up consists of you and people who for some reason won't use public transit.

~~~

Road rage is the expression of the amateur sociopath in all of us, cured by running into a professional.

~~~

Road sign that most applies to life itself: EXPECT DELAYS.

~~~

Evening, and home I go, commuting from a world that doesn't listen to a world that has heard it a thousand times.

Billboards Seen Along The Way

"THREE MILES TO JERRY'S SMELL-THE-ROSES DRIVE-THRU."

"CONTEMPLATIVE RELIGIOUS RETREATS. FREE WI-FI."

"ATTENTION WORKING MOTHERS. TURN YOUR SPARE TIME INTO CASH."

"ENJOY A LEISURELY VACATION IN HALF THE TIME."

"ROAD LESS TRAVELED BY GETAWAYS. HOURLY FLIGHTS FROM ALL MAJOR HUBS."

~~~

<>\<>\<>

Dancing

Keynote Thought

To the optimist, taking a step backward after taking a step forward is not a disaster. It's a cha-cha-cha.

Observations

Dancing is moving to the music without stepping on anyone's toes, pretty much the same as life.

~~~

Ballroom dancing is a meeting of the eyes, with various options for keeping the feet separate.

~~~

With due credit to Ginger Rogers, most women today can dance backwards, in heels, and while talking on a cellphone.

~~~

<>< ><>

Destiny

On a windswept hill
By a billowing sea,
My destiny sits
And waits for me.

Observations

Any intersection can be the corner of Destiny and Chance, any barroom the Karma Lounge of the Serendipity Hotel.

~~~

Every believer in chance is just one chance meeting away from believing in destiny.

~~~

Sometimes Fate brings two people together by causing one to misinterpret a smile.

~~~

It is sad when two people turn from the paths they're following, and their paths go on to cross without them.

~~~

Sometimes in life you have an appointment with destiny, and sometimes you just have to get destiny to squeeze you in.

~~~

Life starts out as partly destiny and partly free will, but then you have kids and it's all destiny.

~~~

Chance has this in common with destiny -- that it is just as apt to be chiseled in stone.

~~~

It is curious that people who profess no belief in destiny still complain of their lot in life.

~~~

We lack resolve and blame fate, mistaking the drift for the tides.

~~~

<><><>

Destiny

Two raindrops, flung from the heavens, merge on a windowpane. Chance meeting? Tell it to the two raindrops.

~~~

It remains an open question -- are we marionettes or are we creatures of free will who just happen to have a lot of jerky reflexes?

Speaking For Myself

Seems like every time I go to the ocean, the tide comes in when I want it to go out -- the sort of luck that has dogged me all my life.

~~~

Alas, by the time Fate caught up with my life, Chance had it all planned.

~~~

Last I heard from my destiny, it wanted me to go one-quarter mile and make a legal U-turn.

~~~

I've lived enough of my life story to know this -- even if Fate writes the book, you make the movie.

~~~

If You Want My Opinion

I don't know that any two people are fated to meet, but I think in some cases Fate stands ready to intervene if they don't.

~~~

I believe that Fate can bring two people together but not necessarily for the purpose of making anything easier.

~~~

When it comes to bringing two people together, Fate gets a lot of credit that ought to go to Mischief.

~~~

A Sad Story

They never met, for she waited each day at the corner of Destiny and Romance, and he hung out at the corner of Main and Elm.

~~~

Driving

Keynote Thought

An object at rest tends to stay at rest, especially if you're behind it when the light turns green.

How True, How True

An important driving aid at my age is someone in the passenger's seat shouting, "Dear God!"

~~~

One advantage of failing eyesight is that you think other drivers are giving you the thumbs-up.

~~~

The most common decision made at the eleventh hour is that we'd better start looking for a motel.

~~~

For every sign that says, "Drive Carefully." shouldn't there be a sign that says, "Resume Normal Driving?"

~~~

Speaking For Myself

"And I, I took the road less traveled by." I was using a GPS system.

~~~

It finally happened. I got the GPS lady so confused that she said, "In one-quarter mile, make a legal stop and ask directions."

~~~

Signs On The Interstate

"FINES DOUBLED NEXT TEN MILES. VARIOUS REASONS."

"TRAFFIC SLOWS AHEAD. NOBODY KNOWS WHY."

"LEAVING WORK ZONE. RESUME EXCESSIVE SPEED."

~~~

<><><>

Emotions

Keynote Thought

Never let your emotions rule, but always let them testify.

Observations

It is a safe bet that anyone who tells you you need to calm down has never actually seen you when you needed to calm down.

~~~

Moral outrage is better worn up your sleeve than on your sleeve.

~~~

In people who change the world, there is a calm that is the storm.

~~~

Why do I sometimes let my emotions get the better of me? For the same reason I let it rain last Tuesday.

~~~

<> <> <>

Entitlement

Keynote Thought

Nothing we feel entitled to ever comes to us in sufficient abundance to make us happy.

Observations

What you find, always, in a happy person is not a sense of entitlement but a feeling of having been blessed.

~~~

Shall you redirect your life's journey because down some side road is some trifle you're entitled to?

~~~

What we earn by the sweat of our brow, we defend with pride. What we gain by the accident of birth, we guard with prejudice.

~~~

Faith

Keynote Thought

Where hope would otherwise become hopelessness, it becomes faith.

Observations

Things happen in life that make us question our faith when perhaps they ought to make us question our life.

~~~

Look at it this way -- if your prayers were always answered, you'd be praying to someone no wiser than you are.

~~~

It is not unreasonable to have faith in that which is necessary for your happiness.

~~~

If you give it a central place in your life, what does it matter if you call it faith or you call it doubt?

~~~

To some, that which cannot be explained is a mystery. To others, that which cannot be explained is the explanation.

~~~

If you listed all the reasons for your faith and all the things that make you cry, it would be essentially the same list.

~~~

It is easier to come to faith from doubt than to return to faith from certainty.

~~~

They are Godseekers both, the churchgoing believer and the pilgrim to an unknown shrine.

~~~

What is certainty but the refuge of those whose faith is not strong enough to entertain doubt?

~~~

No one who has someone to pray for remains long in doubt that there is Someone to pray to.

~~~

Speaking For Myself

*Of course, I doubt. I do not practice a certainty. I
practice a faith.*

~~~

*I believe this -- that to be damned you must travel the
whole wayward journey; to be saved you have only to
start back.*

The Optimist

*The optimist has faith in a loving God, not because it is
the only conceivable faith but because it is the only
conceivable reason for optimism.*

~~~

<><><>

Family

Keynote Thought

*Invariably our days get taken up with family
responsibilities, our search for life's purpose
sidetracked by finding it.*

Observations

*A family is a group of people who keep mistaking you
for someone you were as a kid.*

~~~

*The thing about family disasters is that you never have
to wait long before the next one puts the previous one
into perspective.*

~~~

*There is no family activity so trivial that it doesn't take
your mind off something less important.*

~~~

<>< ><>

Family

In a household of toddler and pets, you can start out having a bad day, but you keep getting sidetracked.

~~~

To say that a family is bound by blood is to underestimate the adhesive power of sweat and tears.

~~~

If minutes were kept of a family meeting, "Members Not Present" and "Subjects Discussed" would be one and the same.

Speaking For Myself

I have never complained of my loved ones taking me for granted, because that was my goal from the start.

~~~

What happens to a member of my family happens to me, which can make for a full day, let me tell you.

~~~

I guess I define "immediate family" as the people who, when you need help, show up immediately.

~~~

Dry, Sly and Wry

Every family has arguments that scare the dog. The concern is when they alarm the cat.

~~~

A common fallacy in large families is that the last person to use it knows where it is.

~~~

Somewhere in everyone's family tree are two people who shouldn't have got married and shouldn't have had kids.

~~~

A family vacation trip is one-third pleasure, fondly remembered, and two-thirds aggravation, entirely forgotten.

~~~

In a household of toddlers and pets, you discover this rule of thumb about happy families -- they are two-thirds incontinent.

~~~

How True, How True

A child never thinks to look for a toy where he last threw it.

~~~

If the older sibling has lost a toy, the younger sibling knows where it is.

~~~

A common parental fallacy is that a lost Scrabble tile has to be somewhere in the house.

~~~

The ideal family board game is one that can be played each time with fewer pieces.

~~~

Life is a series of family photos in which you keep moving to the rear until finally you're a portrait in the background.

~~~

Family life is a bit like a runny peach pie -- not perfect but who's complaining?

~~~

The Family Dictionary

Family: a group of strangers who stick essentially the same nose into each other's business.

Sibling: someone with whom you have nothing in common, frequently mistaken for you.

Cousin: someone you see twice a year, the second time to return the dish.

Nephew, Niece:
someone you always forget is graduating this year.

Great Uncle:
someone at whose funeral you know you're too close to the casket when people keep telling you they're sorry for your loss.

Family Friend:
someone who, as a kid, you never knew who they were except they always brought the macaroni casserole.

Your Own Apartment:
a place where you can be sick in the bathroom at 1 AM without your mother knocking at the door and asking if you're all right.

Fitness

Keynote Thought

The brain forgets much, but the lower back remembers everything.

How True, How True

The way some people treat their bodies, you'd think they were renting.

~~~

It's one thing to accept who you are and another thing to appear in public in such a condition.

~~~

After years of buying clothes I intend to diet into, I'll say this -- the skeleton in my closet has some really nice outfits.

~~~

Of all the pretenses of the cocktail party season, the hardest is pretending that your evening clothes still fit.

~~~

Overheard At The Fitness Center

*"The last straw was when someone called my daughter
a chick off the old blop."*

~~~

*"I have never photographed well, and lately I'm not
reflecting all that well in mirrors."*

~~~

*"So I said to myself, 'There but for the grace of God, go
I,' only to realize I was looking in a mirror and had
seriously overestimated the grace of God."*

~~~

<><><>

Forgiveness

Keynote Thought

If you can't forgive and forget, pick one.

Observations

The beauty of forgiveness is that it requires only a forgiving party. There needn't be a party worthy of forgiveness.

~~~

Often what seems like an unforgiving heart is just time that needs to go by.

~~~

To truly forgive is to let the other person forget.

~~~

If every sin were forgivable, there would be no need for forgiveness.

~~~

Life is too short to hold a grudge, also too long.

~~~

So often when you make the effort to understand, you discover that forgiveness is not required.

~~~

You can build a forgiving relationship on love, but it's harder to build a loving relationship on forgiveness.

~~~

To say, "I love you. Why would I hurt you?" is to ask not for forgiveness but for psychoanalysis.

~~~

It is perhaps unfair to ask forgiveness of love, but that is generally the injured party.

~~~

Some forgive and forget. More forgive and remember. Most forgive and remind.

~~~

Friendship

Keynote Thought

*May you have a good friend to keep you out of trouble --
and a best friend to help you go looking for it.*

Observations

*It is a good friend who tells you a harsh truth, wanting
ten times more to tell you a loving lie.*

~~~

*It is sad to see a friendship expire because you
carelessly assumed it would automatically renew.*

~~~

*You always think you could have done more, which is
why you need a friend -- to tell you you did all you
could.*

~~~

Most of us don't need a psychiatric therapist as much as a friend to be silly with.

~~~

Sometimes it is the person closest to us who must travel the furthest distance to be our friend.

~~~

Our most difficult task as a friend is to offer understanding when we don't understand.

~~~

No matter how sure you are that a friend will be there for you, it's still the greatest feeling when the time comes and there they are.

~~~

Eventually we realize that not all opposing viewpoints come from people who oppose us.

~~~

The best marriages are between two who seek the same God, the best friendships between two who flee the same devil.

~~~

Friendship

A lover is attracted to you physically. A stranger judges you by appearance. Only a friend doesn't give a straw what you look like.

~~~

What do we ask of friendship except to be taken for who we pretend to be -- and without having to pretend.

~~~

There are times in a friendship when one must be friend enough for both.

~~~

Occasionally it's good to reassess those of your friendships in which you are the only participating friend.

If You Want My Advice

Do not be someone looking for friendship. Be friendship looking for someone.

~~~

Today, befriend a stranger, or if you feel up to more of a challenge, befriend a loved one.

~~~

Speaking For Myself

I like friends who, when you tell them you need a moment alone, know enough not to stray too far.

~~~

I value the friend who for me finds time on his calendar, but I cherish the friend who for me does not consult his calendar.

~~~

The thing I've noticed about people with lots of friends is that they don't require a membership.

~~~

It is a good friend who, when I want the truth, knows what truth I want.

Dry, Sly and Wry

We are all the star of our own situation comedy, but occasionally it's great to be the goofy friend in someone else's.

~~~

<><><>

Gardening

Keynote Thought

Overnight it rained, and the wind shifted into the west, and this morning my garden is fresh in the sun, and its scent wafts through my window. But if I sit in my garden, who will keep my appointment in town? But if I keep my appointment in town, who will sit in my garden?

~~~

Observations

Why try to explain miracles to your kids when you can just have them plant a garden?

~~~

If you believe that God is everywhere, then you might well look for Him in a church. But if you wonder if God is anywhere, you might better look for him in a garden.

~~~

In every gardener there is a child who believes in The Seed Fairy.

~~~

A child's garden is a triumph of hope over too much watering.

~~~

What is a gardener but a magician's assistant?

~~~

If you've never experienced the thrill of accomplishing more than you can imagine, plant a garden.

~~~

Speaking For Myself

I sit in my garden, gazing upon a beauty that cannot gaze upon itself, and I find sufficient purpose for my day.

~~~

It pleases me to take amateur photographs of my garden, and it pleases my garden to make my photographs look professional.

~~~

I cultivate my garden, and my garden cultivates me.

~~~

As a gardener I am among those who believe that much of the evidence of God's existence has been planted.

~~~

Does a rose exist that I might behold it, or do I exist that a rose might be beheld?

~~~

I hope some day to meet God, because I want to thank Him for the flowers.

~~~

<>< ><>

God

In many areas of understanding, none so much as in our understanding of God, we bump up against a simplicity so profound that we must assign complexities to it to comprehend it at all. It is mindful of how we paste decals to a sliding glass door to keep from bumping our nose against it.

Observations

God answers first the prayers we should have prayed.

~~~

In nature we see where God has been, In our fellow man we see where He is still at work.

~~~

If God had wanted to be a big secret, He would not have created babbling brooks and whispering pines.

~~~

God

Though we sometimes wonder why God does what He does, we can be sure He does it on better information.

~~~

Many pray to God, but few pray to God for the purpose of hearing a different opinion.

~~~

If life were not so obviously a loan, one might be more inclined to question the existence of a Lender.

~~~

Even if you think the Big Bang created the stars, don't you wonder who sent the flowers?

~~~

To the believer, Creation is God's handiwork. To the scientist, it is just something that happened in the normal course of miracles.

~~~

On the Seventh Day, the Creator sat back, took off His gloves and said, "No fingerprints. They'll just have to find me in the sunsets."

~~~

The most compelling argument that God exists is that the job position so clearly exists.

~~~

Science can reconstruct Tyrannosaurus Rex from a fossilized bone and a fancied footprint but cannot reconstruct God from the whole of Creation?

~~~

Perhaps God, in His wisdom, knew this -- that we would never fully reveal ourselves in prayer to someone we absolutely knew existed.

Speaking For Myself

Sometimes, as practice for convincing myself that God exists, I try to convince my shadow that the sun exists.

A Perspective

There is this about a self-evident truth -- that it can never be proved, because any proof offered will be less self-evident than the premise. All attempts to prove it will appear to fail and, in failing, will cast doubt upon the premise. It is probably so with the existence of God. It is a self-evident truth obscured in the minds of many by dubious proofs.

~~~

<></><>

Gramps & Granny

Keynote Thought

Becoming a grandparent is one of the few pleasures in life for which the consequences have already been paid.

Observations

Life is a process by which, one by one, the trophies on your mantel are replaced by pictures of the grandkids.

~~~

You don't have to train to become a grandparent. Nature just gradually molds you into an entertainment suitable for a younger audience.

~~~

What does a woman wish to be who, finding at her door a small figure with a suitcase, does not wish to be grandmother?

~~~

To a small child, a granddad is someone unafraid of big storms and fierce dogs but absolutely terrified of the word "boo!"

Speaking For Myself

I would gladly go back and travel the road not taken, if I knew at the end of it, I'd find the same set of grandkids.

A Recollection

I remember one Christmas being told that was no Santa Claus, and the next Easter being told that there was no Easter Bunny, and I remember, as Thanksgiving approached, how I feared that they would tell me there was no Grandmother.

~~~

Gratitude

Keynote Thought

There is no such thing as gratitude unexpressed. If it is unexpressed, it is plain old-fashioned ingratitude.

Observations

Any occasion that requires a gift requires an enthusiastic appreciation of the gift.

~~~

It takes a while, but eventually we realize that the people who were always there for the special occasions of our youth had other things to do.

~~~

Always invite into your success the people who helped you get there, for they are the ones most likely to wait for an invitation.

~~~

Grieving

Keynote Thought

Sometimes in tragedy we find our life's purpose -- the eye sheds a tear to find its focus.

Observations

We grieve because we care, and with the passage of time, our consolation is knowing that we cared.

~~~

In the end, the reason for anything is inseparable from the reason for everything.

~~~

It is not until you lose someone you loved too much that you realize you didn't love them too much enough.

~~~

Sometimes a silent hug is the only thing to say.

~~~

Every day is conquerable by its hours and every hour by its minutes.

~~~

A senseless tragedy remains forever tragic, but it is up to us whether it remains forever senseless.

~~~

Yes, people we love die. But it's either that or people dying unloved.

~~~

There comes a time when something you loved no longer is, and what sustains you is knowing that there will never come a time when it no longer was.

Consolation

They seem so fumbling and foolish -- the words of consolation we offer to another. But then one day it becomes our turn to hear them, and how consoling to us those words become and how cherished the friend who stands there, fumbling for them.

~~~

<><><>

Growing Apart

Keynote Thought

So often we don't know what we want, and we blame our unhappiness on someone who doesn't know, either.

Observations

As hard as you try, it is impossible to travel diverging paths by day and meet back at the same place every night

~~~

For want of an occasional expression of love, a relationship strong at the seams can wear thin in the middle.

~~~

It is so hard to realize that a good thing will never be a better thing and still let it be a good thing.

~~~

<>< ><>

Growing Apart

A lovers' quarrel is always about every quarrel you ever had.

~~~

It can be a lifelong battle to love someone through the chinks in their armor.

~~~

If love is to end, it must end in indifference. If it ends in hate, it hasn't ended.

~~~

You can accept a falling-out that changes your plans, but it is harder to accept a betrayal that changes your memories.

~~~

You can as easily love without trusting as you hug without embracing.

~~~

Once there was a couple who parted to go their separate ways, only to discover that they didn't have any ways that were separate.

~~~

<><><>

Halloween

Keynote Thought

There is a child in every one of us who is still a trick-or-treater, looking for a brightly-lit front porch.

Observations

I don't know that there are real ghosts and goblins, but I know that there are always more trick-or-treaters than neighborhood kids.

~~~

Nothing dispels the rattling of ghosts in the attic like the twittering of goblins on the front porch.

~~~

I don't know that there are haunted houses, but I know that there are dark staircases and haunted people.

~~~

Speaking For Myself

I've heard there's been a ghost sighting in my hometown. Come to think of it, I was just back there the other day.

Boo!

There are moonlit nights when the dead send their ghosts to haunt us -- and dark, misty nights when they come themselves.

~~~

For every bodiless spirit you encounter, there's a spiritless body you really don't want to run across.

If You Want My Opinion

Every party is a masquerade party. Even an invitation to come as you are is an invitation to come in your usual disguise.

~~~

<><><>

Happiness

Keynote Thought

Be happy and a reason will come along.

Observations

The trick to being happy is to stop postponing it until such time as you can be happier.

~~~

The key to happiness is to put the burden of proof on unhappiness.

~~~

The ultimate regret is to realize that what you asked of life was never sufficient to make you happy.

~~~

Happiness is a brief glance into how simple it all might be.

~~~

The Search

You can look ahead to happiness, and you can look back on it, but it's so hard to notice it to your left or right.

~~~

The first place to look for happiness is where you left it.

~~~

So often the search for happiness takes you down a familiar street to an old address.

~~~

If you search the world for happiness, you will find it in the end, for the world is round and will lead you back to your door.

~~~

Of all searches, the search for happiness is the most unusual, for we search last in the likeliest places.

~~~

Whatever you set aside to seek happiness, remember where you put it.

~~~

You look for happiness in security, then one day you just say "To heck with it," and you go looking for trouble, and you find happiness.

~~~

It always seems that we would be happier in some faraway place, as if you could hop a plane to a state of mind.

Speaking For Myself

Seeking happiness, I passed many a stranger headed in the opposite direction, seeking happiness.

~~~

Once I saw happiness as a destination and sought a shortcut. Now I see happiness as a road and treasure its every bend.

~~~

I think if we ever succeeded in simplifying our lives, we'd discover that most of our happiness was in the complications.

~~~

<><><>

If You Want My Advice

Be hopeful and happy, and if it proves unwarranted, apologize to anyone you hurt by it.

~~~

Do not ask, "What reason do I have to be happy?" Instead ask, "To what goal can I attach my happiness?"

~~~

Do not spend your life seeking security, and then wonder why you never found happiness.

~~~

Seek out someone who wants to make you happy and let them.

Happiness Is…

Happiness is life served up with a scoop of acceptance, a topping of tolerance and sprinkles of hope, although chocolate sprinkles also work.

~~~

More Observations

Sometimes we don't find the thing that will make us happy because we can't give up the thing that was supposed to.

~~~

It is sad when everything that might make you happy is ever so slightly outside your comfort zone.

~~~

If you are not on your guard, putting on your unhappiness in the morning can become as instinctive as putting on your clothes.

~~~

You can't make someone else happy by making yourself miserable, no matter how diligently you keep up your end of the bargain.

~~~

There is no expert on what happiness is but many on what it might have been.

~~~

Happiness

A true measure of happiness is how many things we get a high from that don't have any street value.

~~~

No matter how carefully you plan your life, your happiness will come down to someone who one day just walked into it.

~~~

To find someone who will love you through success and failure is to discover how little happiness has to do with either.

~~~

You can as easily know the one true recipe for happiness as you can know the one true recipe for shepherd's pie.

~~~

You have to let trivial things make you happy. You can't count on the important things.

~~~

There are two things to know: happiness comes at a price and you have already paid it.

~~~

<><><>

Home and Household

Keynote Thought

We labor to make a house a home, then every time we're expecting visitors, we rush to turn it back into a house.

How True, How True

Always keep your home presentable, assuming you keep a home for purposes of presentation.

~~~

The trouble with, "A place for everything and everything in its place," is that there is always more everything than places.

~~~

Every home has a kitchen drawer organized for knives, forks and spoons and a kitchen drawer organized for dead flashlight batteries, broken corkscrews and used birthday candles.

~~~

<>< ><>

Honor

Keynote Thought

Who would not be a little dishonest, if there were such a thing as a little dishonesty?

Observations

In the end, all the things we acquire by dishonesty are gone, and we are left with only our dishonesty.

~~~

There is an ongoing battle between honor and self-interest in which at some point we have to take sides..

~~~

It is curious how so many feel honor-bound to seek revenge when they never feel honor-bound to do anything else.

~~~

If you hand over your honor on a silver platter, they will want it on gold.

~~~

The one chance to repair a reputation for dishonesty is while you are the only one who knows about it.

~~~

Speaking For Myself

I do not defend my honor. My honor is perfectly able to defend itself. If I'm defending it, it's my pride.

~~~

The phrase, "Duty, Honor, Country" is redundant to this extent -- that if you attend to your duty and honor, you have fully discharged your obligation to country.

~~~

Hope

Keynote Thought

Never lose hope, because miracles happen, and they need something to work with.

Observations

Hope is not a plan, unless hope is all you have left -- then it's a plan.

~~~

Hope is a path through a flowering meadow. One does not require that it lead anywhere.

~~~

There is always sufficient reason for despair, but there is never sufficient purpose.

~~~

You might as well hope for the best, since hoping for less doesn't seem to improve the results any.

~~~

What you have to realize about a hopeless situation is that it's just a situation -- you are supplying the hopelessness.

~~~

Despair is nearly always a still shot, taken from a movie that is not over.

~~~

If hope and despair were paths to the same destination, which would you choose?

~~~

They say it's never too late, but sometimes it is, and you have to wait a day or two before it isn't again.

~~~

Through the darkest night, morning gently tiptoes, feeling its way to dawn.

~~~

Few are hopeless who can look ahead in this world, and no one is hopeless who can look beyond it.

~~~

A shattered dream is like broken glass -- you never quite sweep up all the pieces.

Speaking For Myself

There are spring days when my winter despair seems an offense against the Creator and my black mood an affront to the blue sky.

~~~

Why chase a hopeless dream? I dunno, maybe for the dream, maybe for the chase, maybe to meet another hopeless dreamer.

~~~

There is a state of denial called hope, which I prefer to the state of denial called despair.

~~~

If You Want My Advice

Toss your dashed hopes not into a trash bin but into a drawer where you are likely to rummage some bright morning.

~~~

Never mind that your actions seem hopeless. Act nevertheless, for you have a greater ability to act than to judge hopelessness.

~~~

Dream small that your dreams may come true. Dream large that you might always have a dream.

The Inner Yearning

No matter what you accomplish in life, a part of you still sits at a curbside, still hearing the drumbeat of a distant parade, still waiting for it to turn the corner.

The Ultimate Hope

The lesson of Good Friday is to never lose hope -- or at least give it the weekend.

~~~

<>‹›‹›

Humankind

Keynote Thought

Which of us is not a wanderer in this world, convinced that everyone else knows where they're going.

Observations

The conclusion, "Nobody cares," is always based on an insufficient sampling.

~~~

To know the innermost fears of anyone is to know the innermost fears of everyone.

~~~

Eventually you come to realize that most people aren't looking for a fight but for someone to surrender to.

~~~

No two people are alike. It takes three or more.

~~~

<>

<>

<>

It is hard to decide whether people are the same in different ways or different in the same ways.

~~~

We envy others, for we see their lives in broad outline while forced to live ours in every detail.

~~~

No one passes you on the street who was not once beautiful in someone's eyes.

~~~

We accept the weakness in others that makes them just like us, but we deplore the weakness in ourselves that makes us just like them.

~~~

You discover this -- that when you leave behind your preconceived notions of people, you rarely go back for them.

~~~

It is true of most human beings that if they had no physical body, they would still have an identifying scar.

~~~

People aren't ignoring you. They are busy with their lives, and the way to stop feeling ignored is to get busy with yours.

~~~

Life is a series of events so arranged that if you don't know what someone else is going through, you will soon enough.

~~~

Perhaps God will pity a creature that sought its better angels but found only its lesser demons.

~~~

Nothing brings people together like having the same deck stacked against them.

~~~

Nobody's perfect, and our fondest memories of anyone are of the hilarious ways they proved it.

~~~

The most deserving cries for help are never heard because they are never uttered.

~~~

<><><>

If You Want My Advice

Never point a finger where you never lent a hand.

~~~

Never say that someone does not deserve mercy. Mercy is never deserved. If it were, it would be justice.

The Voice Of Experience

The most fundamental winning formula is to bet on human decency and be patient.

~~~

The people in your life who don't need an invitation still like to get one.

~~~

It's a tricky word -- "everybody." When you hear, "Everybody's doing it," it never includes you, and when you think, "Everybody knows that," it never includes anybody else.

~~~

Humankind

All it takes sometimes to find the silver lining is to remember that it's not all about you.

~~~

Speaking For Myself

I don't know what it takes to be you, and you don't know what it takes to be me, and so we tend to underrate each other's courage.

~~~

I don't know if we're all God's children, but I know if I am, you are.

~~~

On the one hand, I'd like to expect the best from every human being I meet. On the other hand, that would make me a cocker spaniel.

~~~

While I find that I can keep my nose out of other people's business, I do have a curiosity as to their non-business activities.

~~~

<>< ><>

Humankind

Dry, Sly and Wry

Don't look at it as my right to privacy. Look at it as your right to mind your own business.

~~~

On the Sixth Day, God created man, the sort of result you get when you go into work on the weekend.

~~~

Once there was an animal who was sent to fetch but could never figure out who sent him or what for.

~~~

The human species is made up of seven billion subspecies, each consisting of one specimen.

~~~

Human beings -- just when you think you know what makes them tick, they tock.

~~~

It is possible to find something good in everyone. The trick is to stop right there.

~~~

123

Humility

Keynote Thought

There is a quiet, unassuming pride that no misfortune can humble, and it goes by the name of humility.

Observations

Few are humble, for it requires a self-esteem few possess.

~~~

One learns to ignore criticism by first learning to ignore applause.

~~~

To inspire awe in anyone should inspire embarrassment in ourselves.

~~~

The first thing to suspect in those who admire us is flawed judgment.

~~~

The Voice of Experience

If you could eavesdrop on everything said about you, you'd spend most of your time waiting for the subject to come up.

Speaking For Myself

It's not that I'm this larger-than-life figure; it's that I've had this smaller-than-I-figured life.

~~~

I have been humbled by praise, and I have been humbled by whiffing on the first tee, and somehow it's different.

~~~

I make no claim to fame, realizing that it would probably end up in small claims court anyway.

~~~

And as a last request, I have asked for whatever style tombstone will make the mowing easier.

~~~

<><><>

Judging Others

Keynote Thought

Always carry with you a little reasonable doubt, should you meet someone who needs to be found innocent.

Observations

Sometimes the best exercise of good judgment is knowing when to withhold your better judgment.

~~~

The key to compassion is to realize that everyone you meet is a set of extenuating circumstances.

~~~

Most people are better than we judge, for we do not know the temptations they have overcome.

~~~

Sometimes, to make the right judgment, you have to be too involved to be impartial.

~~~

It is hard to see ourselves from the other person's point of view -- and harder to see the other person from the other person's point of view.

If You Want My Advice

Never confuse having all the facts with knowing the whole story.

~~~

Be reluctant to judge, for it's hard to know another person's true intent -- or the true intent of the judge.

~~~

*Always when judging
Who people are,
Remember to footnote
The words, "So far."*

~~~

Judging Ourselves

Keynote Thought

A moment we never forget is the first time we found the courage not to blame ourselves.

Observations

Nobody's perfect, in case you thought you were perfect, or in case you thought you were nobody.

~~~

Life is a series of events that happen in such a way that it seems to be your fault.

~~~

There's no need to take the blame for every fool thing that ever happened -- and it's too early anyway.

~~~

Life is a game of dominoes in which every domino blames itself.

~~~

Self-criticism is always an attempt to head off hearing it from someone else, who otherwise would never have given it a thought.

———

The thing about letting yourself be victimized is that it's so hard to blame the right person.

If You Want My Advice

Stay out of the court of self-judgment, for there is no presumption of innocence.

Speaking For Myself

The verdict is still out on my life, the judge having not yet instructed the jury, both of whom are me.

~~~

<><><>

Justice

Keynote Thought

Life is not fair, nor has it ever been, but the morning seems determined to dawn until it is.

Observations

You know something's wrong with the system when you find yourself begging for justice as if it were mercy.

~~~

The battle now and always is to ensure that justice remains admissible in a court of law.

~~~

Justice delayed is justice denied. It is vengeance that tends to be administered promptly.

~~~

Better to serve a just God and discover He is forgiving than to serve a forgiving God and discover He is just.

~~~

<><><>

Kids

The world is as many times new as there are children in our lives.

Observations

A child seldom needs a good talking-to as much as a good listening-to.

~~~

If we would listen to our kids, we'd find that they are largely self-explanatory.

~~~

Kids do not follow our preachings; they follow us.

~~~

Before you discourage a child, recall your own childhood, and ask yourself what damage to your self-confidence you now believe was temporary.

~~~

Kids

The world knows how to straighten out a spoiled child, but never makes it up to a child deprived.

~~~

A question to ask, as parent or teacher, is whether a child who never won your approval ever knew it was available.

~~~

You can teach kids to know better, but you can't teach them not to do it anyway.

~~~

When kids feel they have won our respect, the last thing they want is our unconditional love.

~~~

Yes, it's a tired old world, but a kid can still find six fascinating detours from the school bus to the front door.

~~~

The tragedy of a sad child is that a child has such a capacity to be cheered up.

~~~

Kids grow up whether you raise them or not, generally spending a lot more time growing up than being raised,

~~~

Dry, Sly and Wry

One thing an adult can learn from a kid is when to pick up your marbles and go home.

~~~

No kid enters his or her teen years with a well thought out exit strategy.

~~~

Whether you think a kid likes you or hates you depends pretty much on your interpretation of blank looks.

~~~

It is difficult to understand kids, because their minds are undeveloped while ours are still undeveloping.

~~~

Kid to kid: "I don't get my mom. She expects me to know why I want to do something before I even do it."

~~~

Learning

If there's one thing I know for sure, but, alas, there isn't.

Observations

Learning is a lifetime process, but at some point you have to stop adding and start updating.

~~~

Looking back, you realize that everything would have explained itself if you had only stopped interrupting.

~~~

It's a mistake, when life hands you a hard lesson, to think you can get back at life by not learning it.

~~~

If you keep rephrasing the question, it gradually becomes the answer.

~~~

It's amazing what you can learn by listening to people you don't want to hear it from.

~~~

You only stop getting wiser when there's nothing left to learn too late.

~~~

The hardest thing about becoming knowledgable is that you have to give up certainty.

~~~

The trouble with thinking you're 100% right is that it's the only way you can be 100% wrong.

~~~

The first requirement of learning is to have absolutely no idea what you want to hear.

~~~

There are several ways to become an expert, self-appointment being the most common.

~~~

The mind has this in common with the body -- that it needs a regular bowel movement.

~~~

<><><>

Learning

It's a shame to trade your youthful curiosity for a bunch of answers that make you wonder why you were ever curious.

~~~

Wisdom is not what you know but how quickly you adjust when the opposite proves true.

~~~

If You Want My Advice

Every day learn something new, and just as important, relearn something old.

~~~

Speaking For Myself

Oh, if I had known yesterday what I know today. And remind me again -- what is it that I know today?

~~~

I've concluded after many years that my mind works by process of elimination. Problem is, it hasn't eliminated anything yet.

~~~

If I had it to do again, I'd ask more questions and interrupt fewer answers.

~~~

There are truths of which I have an inkling, but of most I have only a penciling.

School Days

Too often the first thing a child learns in school is to stop asking questions that can't be answered.

~~~

The average teacher explains complexity; the gifted teacher reveals simplicity.

~~~

The difference between education and know-how is that one you pay for, the other you charge for.

~~~

Life

Keynote Thought

Why be saddled with this thing called life expectancy? Of what relevance to an individual is such a statistic? Am I to concern myself with an allotment of days I never had and was never promised? Must I check off each day of my life as if I am subtracting from this imaginary hoard? No, on the contrary, I will add each day of my life to my treasure of days lived. And, with each day, my treasure will grow, not diminish.

~~~

<>　<><>

Life

Observations

Life is the chance you've been waiting for.

~~~

We complain that life is not easy. But did we pray for an easy life, or did we pray for happiness and fulfillment -- and did we suppose it would be easy?

~~~

What to do with your one life? The same thing you would do if you had two lives, and this were the second.

~~~

As you wait for better days, don't forget to enjoy today -- in case they've already started.

~~~

Occasionally ask, "What is the connection between what I want most in life and anything I plan to do today?"

~~~

God sends the dawn
That we might see
The might-have-beens
That still might be.

~~~

139

<><><>

Life begins when you stop making excuses and find yourself a reason.

~~~

Maybe you never catch the dream you chase all your life, but it usually takes you up the road you want to travel.

~~~

What you discover about a dream come true is that you must keep dreaming it to make it stay true.

~~~

The more side roads you stop to explore, the less likely that life will pass you by.

~~~

You don't want to get to the end of life's journey and discover that you never left the interstate.

~~~

There are people who live their whole lives on the default setting, never realizing that you can customize.

~~~

Life is short, God's way of encouraging a bit of focus.

~~~

May it be said of you that you relished the dance of life and went out applauding the band.

~~~

If you never pause to look about you, it is possible to live a dull gray life under a blue sky.

~~~

You have a claim on life, and at some point life will offer you a settlement. Don't take it.

~~~

In childhood we yearn to be grown-ups. In old-age, we yearn to be kids. It just seems that all would be wonderful if we didn't have to celebrate our birthdays in chronological order.

~~~

If you don't decide what your life is about, it defaults to what you spend your days doing.

~~~

There is a purpose to our lives that each day tugs at our sleeve as an annoying distraction.

~~~

<><><>

If You Want My Advice

*Do things while you can, and while they matter to you,
because neither is a permanent state of affairs.*

~~~

*Get involved. You don't want to reach the end of your
life and discover that you successfully managed to stay
out of it.*

~~~

*Always keep a list of priorities, but occasionally start
from the bottom.*

~~~

*Never be surprised if what must inevitably happen
happens right now.*

~~~

*Do not ask little of life and then wonder why it gives you
nothing.*

~~~

Never say never, and never, ever, say never ever.

~~~

Speaking For Myself

I want to thank God for my life, which is to say, for this brief opportunity to explain myself.

~~~

I count myself lucky, having long ago won a lottery paid to me in seven sunrises a week for life.

~~~

I don't so much regret the road not taken as my all-fired hurry along the road I took.

~~~

I think my life would make a great TV movie. It even has the part where they say, "Stand by. We are experiencing temporary difficulties."

~~~

I have long suspected that life is a distraction, but I've never been able to figure out from what.

~~~

Things happen in everyday life that make you consider living your life just every other day.

~~~

<><><>

Ask Yourself This

If you could apply for a life of ease, what exactly would you state as the purpose of your request?

~~~

Will you spend your life pushing a boulder uphill so that, once uphill, you will have a boulder to sit on while regretting your life?

How True, How True

Sometimes your life seems like a furniture arrangement where everything is where you told the delivery guy to leave it for now.

~~~

Ever get the feeling that some time early in your life there was a briefing you missed?

~~~

Life never tires of testing the proposition that life must go on.

~~~

Still More Observations

Life is an educational process you can't opt out of. You either learn the lesson, or you become the lesson.

~~~

You can live your life so as not to rock the boat, but you could have done that by not being born.

~~~

Whatever life is, it is not a test to see how quickly you can attain your dream by spending your every waking hour on something else.

~~~

It is said that you only get one life. Truth is, you only get one birth and one death. How many lives you squeeze in is up to you.

~~~

At some point you just have to let heredity and environment debate themselves while you go off and shape your own life.

~~~

Life is all about discovering things that do matter in the end.

~~~

Life Is...

Life is a collection of moments you might have appreciated more if you had only known they were moments.

~~~

Life is a series of stages, each preparation for the previous.

~~~

Life is a grand party where you never get to meet the host and have to leave when others are just arriving.

~~~

Life is a vale of tears where at times you just can't stop giggling.

~~~

Life is a set of reactions that aren't what you intend -- to a set of situations that aren't what they seem.

~~~

Life is like a fancy restaurant -- it will always try to seat you at the worst table you will accept.

~~~

Life is like sailing. You can use any wind to go in any direction.

Once Heard

"They were happy days, those days of struggle. I know it now, and what I will always thank God for, I knew it then."

You Be The Quotesmith

When you get right down to it, only three things are necessary in life: faith, family and an occasional--

Take Your Pick

cold beer
cup of tea
glass of wine
walk in the woods
stroll on the beach
shopping spree
pepperoni pizza
your choice.

~~~

Listening

Keynote Thought

I have learned to just quietly listen, finding it is usually what people want when they ask for my input.

Observations

The first thing to learn about the art of conversation is that you are not the other person's favorite subject.

~~~

You never have another person's fuller attention than when you're listening to them.

~~~

The advantage of silence over words is that there's a wider range of things you can claim you didn't mean by it.

~~~

A pleasant smile is the wisest comment, always interpreted favorably and rarely misquoted.

~~~

There was never an embarrassing silence that couldn't be turned into a regrettable conversation.

~~~

So many things go through your mind that you never say. So many things you say never go through your mind.

~~~

It's amazing the ideas that pop into your head while someone is saying them into your ear.

~~~

The way to argue with an articulate person is to respond with a silence and let them articulate it.

If You Want My Advice

Learn to hold your tongue, and you will be fluent in every language and on all topics.

~~~

Better to stand there with a blank look on your face than to utter words to that effect.

~~~

Loneliness

Keynote Thought

Nightfall, and the lonely crowd disperses to become lonely separately.

Observations

In the end, who among us does not choose to be a little less right to be a little less lonely.

~~~

Perhaps we misjudge other people's loneliness because we are so seldom with them when they're alone.

~~~

It is a good friend who respects your solitude but won't let your loneliness have a moment alone.

~~~

If God had intended us to be alone, there would be more pleasure in massaging our own shoulders.

~~~

There are lonely days, when the mind recalls promises not kept, and lonely nights, when the heart recalls promises not made.

~~~

Speaking For Myself

I have been alone in a crowd. In fact, I have more than once sought a crowd for that very purpose.

~~~

In my loneliest dream, I am alone on a station platform, having missed the last train to eternity.

Line From An Unfinished Novel

"She lived alone, kept company by a dog that never barked and a phone that never rang."

~~~

<>< ><>

Love

Keynote Thought

Love demands, Friendship asks;

Love drains, Friendship refreshes;

Love is jealous, Friendship is tolerant;

Love constrains, Friendship frees;

Love wants more, Friendship takes what it gets.

Love sits by your bedside through the long night of illness;
Friendship pops in for a visit.

~~~

Observations

We never give up wanting things for ourselves, but there comes a day when what we want for ourselves is someone else's happiness.

~~~

You know you've found love when you can't find your way back.

~~~

We picture love as heart-shaped because we do not know the shape of the soul.

~~~

In life you start out knowing nothing and end up knowing better. In love you start out knowing better and end up knowing nothing.

~~~

Love is at first a set of romantic fancies that as the years go by you discard like training wheels, and you learn to love truly.

~~~

<><><>

Love

It is not necessary to be strong in every place if in the place you are vulnerable, you are loved.

~~~

Sometimes the shortest distance between two points is a winding path walked arm-in-arm.

~~~

It's true love when, hard as you try, you can't think of any way to use it to your advantage.

~~~

Is it so much that love asks -- that one day you be its strength and the next day its babe-in-arms?

~~~

What we seek in our lives is not unconditional love but a love for which we, uniquely in all the world, meet all the conditions.

~~~

Love is not about grand intentions; it is about small attentions.

~~~

How True, How True

It's love when the world stands still, and it is you who are spinning on your axis.

~~~

You know it's true love when reality sets in, and it doesn't change a thing.

~~~

Sometimes love is just a comfort in each other's presence that shows up as long silences on the interstate.

~~~

The hardest thing to learn in the game of love is when to fold a winning hand.

~~~

Love may be blind, but like most who are blind, it knows pretty much where everything is.

~~~

Yes, there are reasons no one could ever love you, and you can be sure your lover knows them all.

~~~

<><><>

Love

The heart has its reasons, and they aren't debate topics.

~~~

No one ever falls in love for the purpose of debating the wisdom of the move.

~~~

Love is the greatest touch-up artist of all.

~~~

There is more love at second glance than at first sight.

If You Want My Advice

While debating the question, "What is love?", yield to all desperate desires to make someone happy.

~~~

Some say that true love is a mirage. Seek it anyway, for all else is surely desert.

~~~

Before you pledge your undying love to someone, make them promise they won't die.

~~~

Those Three Little Words

It is so simple a sentiment, "I love you," and yet so hard sometimes to get the wording right.

~~~

It's a bit too late, after you say, "I love you," to start parsing out the promises not included.

~~~

It's generally a good idea not to say "I love you" if there's something you don't mean by it.

~~~

There are people who can't say, "I love you." They can only say, "I miss you."

~~~

It's curious the way a person can say, "She sells seashells by the seashore," and can't say, "I love you."

~~~

A good speech has a beginning, a middle and an end, the best example being, "I love you."

~~~

Love

Still More Observations

In the eyes of love we are beautiful, and even more astonishing, we are lovable!

~~~

Love is given to us as a time, but to keep it always, we must make it a place.

~~~

If you could be the perfect person your lover imagines, what would be the point of love?

~~~

Being loved by all is little fun,
Unless you're also loved by one.

~~~

It is not given to the human heart to love less in order to love equally.

~~~

Only in love can you be blindsided by something you saw coming.

~~~

To fall in love is not to enter the world of our dreams but to find someone who will take us by the hand and lead us out of it.

~~~

Love can be a conversation about nothing -- or it can be a quiet moment that is about everything.

~~~

It isn't sad enough when love dies; we must torture ourselves with the thought that it never was.

~~~

No one complains of being a prisoner of love who has ever been a prisoner of loneliness.

~~~

So often our loved ones mistake our understanding for approval, having already mistaken our love for understanding.

~~~

You can as easily stop caring as you can go back and not start.

~~~

<><><>

Marriage

Keynote Thought

Marriage is the unforeseen consequence of marrying for love.

Observations

There comes a time when two people realize that their separate schemes can be better achieved as a conspiracy.

~~~

To be true to one another is not merely a promise. There are times in a marriage when it's your only plan.

~~~

There is basically just one marriage vow, and that is to be the person your partner thinks they're marrying.

~~~

Two things are owed to truthfulness -- lasting marriages and short friendships.

~~~

How to make a marriage last? You work at it every day, and once a year you celebrate the anniversary of the same wedding.

~~~

The hardest thing in marriage is to trust after having been certain.

~~~

Most marriages can survive better or worse. The tester is all those years of exactly the same.

Speaking For Myself

The older I get, the less time I want to spend with the part of the human race that didn't marry me.

~~~

It's comforting to have a partner who can finish my sentences, even if she doesn't finish them the way I would.

~~~

How True, How True

Most often the person for whom you would climb any mountain and swim any sea would settle for a little conversation at dinner.

~~~

One thing you learn in a long marriage is how many sneezes to wait before saying, "Bless you."

~~~

Love is blind, but it isn't deaf. It can turn plainness into beauty, but it can't turn snoring into a good night's sleep.

~~~

Marriage has this in common with riding a Brahma bull -- it is judged less by style points than duration.

The Two Musketeers

"Each for the other and two against the world."

~~~

Dry, Sly and Wry

The wedding is where two become one. The marriage is where they decide which one.

~~~

One thing a man discovers in marriage is that there's nothing easier than pleasing your wife with your cooking.

~~~

The reason that everyone's smiling in wedding photos is that it's based on the information they had at the time.

~~~

Say what you want about marriage, it's still the best known cure for unnecessary conversation.

If You Want My Advice

Never marry anyone that you can't picture helping you go to the bathroom.

~~~

<> <> <>

Memories

Keynote Thought

There are memories I choose not to live with, but we hang out at the same bar.

Observations

The happiest memories are of moments that ended when they should have.

~~~

There are memories that will always make you lonesome but will never make you sad.

~~~

Nostalgia -- we live our days in the glare of the sun and remember them in the glow of the moon.

~~~

Not everything has to happen to be fondly recalled.

~~~

It's curious the way we get nostalgic for a dream that never came true, as if a dream that never came true were in the past.

Speaking For Myself

l enjoy, occasionally, a day with my memories -- these paintings hanging on the walls of my mind.

~~~

I am grateful for all memories, so much of my life having escaped my attention altogether.

~~~

*Recalling days of sadness, memories haunt me.
Recalling days of happiness, I haunt my memories.*

A Reminiscence

*Under every full moon,
I recall a lagoon
Where a mandolin played,
And memories stir
Of the dreamers we were
And the plans that we made.*

~~~

<>‹›‹>

Miracles

Keynote Thought

You can hope for a miracle in your life, or you can see your life as the miracle.

Observations

There are times when you don't need a miracle, but you definitely need something unknown to science.

~~~

When a miracle happens, it is usually in the near proximity of someone who believed it would.

~~~

The difference between a miracle and luck is that you can have luck without believing in it.

~~~

If you don't believe in miracles, it is wise to marry someone who does.

~~~

Speaking For Myself

I believe there's an explanation for everything, so, yes, I believe in miracles.

~~~

It strikes me as just crazy not to believe in the miracles your happiness depends on.

If You Want My Advice

If you don't believe in miracles, pray. And if you don't believe in prayer, pray for a miracle.

~~~

<><><>

Mom

Keynote Thought

If you have a mom, there is nowhere you are likely to go where a prayer has not already been.

Observations

What is a mom but the sunshine of our days and the north star of our nights.

~~~

Conscience is less an inner voice than the memory of a mother's glance.

~~~

Through both their lives, a mom never stops chasing her child down to the water's edge.

~~~

There is little you achieve whose possibility was not first exaggerated by your mom.

~~~

<><><>

Mom

There seems, early in life, to be countless reasons for happiness, and then you discover your mom is making them up.

~~~

A mom sees past your excuses to the real reason it's not your fault.

~~~

A mom knows all our hiding places, beginning with the very first.

~~~

A mom's hopes always exceed her expectations, and her encouragement always exceeds her hopes.

~~~

If loving you less would make you happy, do you suppose your mom wouldn't try?

~~~

Eventually you realize that the reason God didn't always answer your prayers is that He was answering your mom's prayers.

~~~

<>< ><>

Mom

*All we ask of our mom is to rejoice when we find
someone who can make us happier than she can.*

~~~

*Mom is the only relative you can appeal to who will
never look upon it as an appeal to your relationship.*

~~~

*Sometimes, in a moral struggle, we remember a lesson
our mother taught us, just as on a cold winter's day
long ago, we discovered mittens pinned to our coat
sleeves.*

Hide and Seek

*A mother always counts to ten,
And never, never peeks,
But always knows just where you hide,
And there she never seeks
Until the very nick of time
Lest tears run down your cheeks.*

~~~

Eventually you realize that your mom knows exactly who you are and has been trying to break it to you gently all your life.

~~~

Every woman knows how to play the single mom and does so exactly to the extent her marriage requires.

~~~

Overheard: *"The best friend I ever had was not trying to be my friend. She was trying to be my dad."*

How True, How True

A mom forgives you all your faults, not to mention one or two you don't even have.

~~~

A mom reads you like a book, and wherever she goes, people read you like a glowing book review.

~~~

Mom

Speaking For Myself

The words of my first confession, "I disobeyed my mother," would suffice for every sin I have committed since.

~~~

All I know about life is that it was the first thing my mom ever volunteered me for.

~~~

I guess I have never doubted that we are all born to our guardian angels.

~~~

Whenever I see a lost person and think, "There but for the grace of God go I," I realize that the grace of God was my mom.

~~~

<><><>

Morality

Keynote Thought

Nothing in life is so little appreciated as the moral character it takes to be a normal, everyday person.

Observations

There is a final stage in the relaxation of morals where everything is offensive but it doesn't offend anyone.

~~~

Two wrongs don't make a right, but some folks seem hellbent on finding out how many wrongs will.

~~~

As a general guideline, it is good to avoid actions that would be lying and cheating if somebody else did them.

~~~

You must question a code of ethics that never impedes your progress.

~~~

Morality

There are things you've done that come back to haunt you -- and things that haunt you that you're still doing.

~~~

What you need to know about the offer Satan made to Christ in the desert is that he makes it to everybody.

~~~

What good is a moral code that causes you to regret but never causes you to reconsider?

~~~

How do you become a good person? You practice the mannerisms until they become your own.

~~~

The best evidence that you are doing the right thing is that it isn't easy.

~~~

The list keeps growing -- the evils condoned by otherwise good people -- until one day there's no otherwise left.

~~~

Speaking For Myself

I am less motivated by people urging me to do the right thing than by people assuming I will.

~~~

All I ask of anyone judging my sins is that they consider the sins I was capable of.

~~~

Called to do good, I protest that I am but one person. Tempted to do evil, I reckon that one person should be sufficient.

~~~

The one thing I would guess about the Lord of Judgment is that He probably won't blame your parents.

~~~

I do believe in accountability. It satisfies not just the moralist in me but the accountant in me.

~~~

<><><>

Opportunity

Keynote Thought

*Opportunity is a parade. No sooner does one chance
pass than the next is a fife and drum in the distance.*

Observations

*You do not seize an opportunity. You seize a moment
and create an opportunity.*

~~~

*As you seek new opportunity, keep in mind that the sun
does not usually reappear on the horizon where last
seen.*

~~~

*There is always a new day. You ride off into the sunset
and discover it's the sunrise.*

~~~

*Life is a thousand opportunities, more if that isn't
enough.*

~~~

A question to occasionally ask yourself is what you would do if you had tomorrow to live over again.

~~~

It is a sad lament -- the happiness you might have found if you had taken the path that still lies right there in front of you.

~~~

What can be sadder than to realize that you had the key but never tried the lock.

If You Want My Advice

Seize every moment along the way, for what a shame it would be if the road you chose became the road not taken.

Speaking For Myself

If I were Opportunity, I wouldn't just knock -- you'd have to sign.

~~~

Optimism

Keynote Thought

The optimist doesn't know whether life is a comedy or a tragedy. He's just tickled silly to be in the play.

Observations

The average pencil is seven inches long with just a half-inch eraser, in case you thought optimism was dead.

~~~

How many times must the sun rise before a pessimist realizes it's going to keep doing it?

~~~

God created an endless day with intervals of light and darkness. It is the optimist who created tomorrow.

~~~

In life's poker game, the optimist sees the pessimist's night and raises him the sunrise.

~~~

To be a pessimist in this world is to sit by a stream of golden nuggets and pan for sludge.

~~~

How do you tell an optimist that he or she has lived a happy life by mistake?

~~~

It can be said of optimism that while sometimes mistaken, it is never sadly mistaken.

~~~

An optimist realizes that when everyone seems to doubt you, it's just everyone you've met so far.

~~~

Optimism is the knack of not letting every conceivable thing that could ruin your life ruin your day.

~~~

Beethoven composed symphonies after becoming deaf. Monet painted masterpieces after becoming blind. The pessimist hears this and thinks, "With my luck, I'll never go deaf or blind."

~~~

Speaking For Myself

I think there would be a lot more optimists if it weren't for the rise-and-shine requirement.

~~~

It's still possible to be a cockeyed optimist these days. You just have to be a little more cockeyed.

Define Optimist

An optimist is someone who figures that if it walks like a duck and quacks like a duck, it's the bluebird of happiness.

The Voice of Optimism

"I know he's still alive, because he doesn't call and he doesn't write, which is just like him."

Dry, Sly and Wry

Obituary in The Daily Optimist: "In lieu of flowers, send smelling salts."

~~~

<><><>

Parenting

There is no scientific theory of the universe that sufficiently answers the question, "Who entrusted to me this child?"

Observations

A parent's love is whole no matter how many times divided.

~~~

When you bring up kids, there are memories you store directly in your tear ducts.

~~~

The most persistent false notion in parenting is that something is happening somewhere else that you are missing out on.

~~~

<>< ><>

Define Parenthood

*Parenthood is the passing of a baton, followed by a
lifelong disagreement as to who dropped it.*

~~~

*Parenthood is a stage of life's journey where the
milestones come about every fifty feet.*

~~~

If life is theater, parenting is improv.

~~~

*Parenting is the realization that of all the lives you might
have lived, only one was ever really possible.*

Speaking For Myself

*In a dark moment I ask, "How can anyone bring a child
into this world?" And the answer rings clear, "Because
there is no other world, and because the child has no
other way into it."*

~~~

I say to my child, "I will explain to you as much of life as I can, but you must understand that there is a part of life for which you are the explanation."

~~~

"How, child, do I know where you're headed? Because I'm there, and I can see you coming."

The Voice of Experience

What you must accept as a parent is that you can't always be there for your child without sometimes ruining everything.

~~~

It is one thing to show your child the way, and a harder thing to then stand out of it.

~~~

The trouble with learning to parent on the job is that your child is the teacher.

~~~

<><><>

Parenting

There are days as a parent when you would feel trapped and overwhelmed if it weren't so beside the point.

~~~

It is only when we have a child we cannot love enough that we realize why our parents loved us too much.

~~~

The trouble with having a stubbornness contest with your kids is that they have your stubbornness gene.

~~~

The clash between child and adult is never so stubborn as when the child in us confronts the adult in our child.

~~~

As parents, we guide by our unspoken example. It is only when we're talking to them that our kids aren't listening.

~~~

There are days when you'd just like to enter the world of your child's imagination and never return.

~~~

What makes raising a child so difficult is that each day you must start with the child you have raised so far.

~~~

Yes, to be a good parent you have to make sacrifices, but that is not a requirement of parenting, it is a requirement of being good at something.

~~~

Anything we tell our kids about life is a placemarker until they figure it out for themselves.

If You Want My Advice

If you teach your kids nothing else, teach them the Golden Rule and "righty-tighty, lefty-loosey."

~~~

Do not ask that your kids live up to your expectations. Let your kids be who they are, and your expectations will be in breathless pursuit.

~~~

Dry, Sly and Wry

Raising kids is a series of mistakes it is critical to make at the recommended age.

~~~

You try to raise kids who are secure in your love and certain of their next meal, which, let's face it, doesn't leave you a whole lot of leverage.

~~~

To use a baseball analogy, seeing your kids safely into their beds each night is hitting a homerun -- and doing it 6500 times or more gets you into the Parenting Hall of Fame.

~~~

The parent-child relationship is unique in that the parent does all the favors and the child holds all the IOU's.

~~~

Parenting is an amateur activity that requires professional cleaning.

~~~

<><><>

Passage

Keynote Thought

When I am gone, my love, do not look for me in the places we used to go to together. Look for me in the places we always planned to go to together.

When Death Comes For Us

When Death comes for us,
May our lives be safely stored away
In the minds and hearts of all we have loved
And in the happiness and well-being
Of all we have helped,
And may Death find no life to take from us,
But shuffle off defeated,
Having relieved us only of our dying.

~~~

Overheard at a Gravesite

And they all said "I'm sorry for your loss," as if you were someone who could ever be taken from me.

Observations

The thing about people who understand you is that when they die, you can still visit them, and they still understand you.

~~~

You don't realize how much you depend on someone until they die -- and you go to tell them the news.

Speaking For Myself

I've thought about living and dying, and I think it's probably better than living and being left behind.

~~~

<><><>

Perseverance

Keynote Thought

How often in life we complete a task that was beyond the capability of the person we were when we started it.

Observations

There are times when you just have to look in the mirror and say, "I will if you will."

~~~

May it be said of you that you had your shortcomings but being stopped by your shortcomings wasn't one of them.

~~~

Two things are needed to succeed -- a sensible plan and a willingness to stick to it when any sensible person would give up.

~~~

<><><>

Perseverance

We find in ourselves the strength to overcome every obstacle, which is a good thing, because we also find in ourselves every obstacle.

~~~

We gain no greater advantage than by relentlessly pursuing our goal while others pursue an advantage.

~~~

As a means to success, perseverance has this advantage over talent -- that it doesn't have to be recognized by others.

~~~

Genius is a plodding intellect, incapable of dreaming up the obstacles that stop the rest of us.

~~~

What shall I be -- the angry sea
That pounds against the shore,
Or soft agleam, the quiet stream
That carves the canyon floor?

~~~

If You Want My Advice

Never demand, never beg. Be like a river seeking the sea -- politely insist.

~~~

Stubbornly persist, and you find that the limits of your stubbornness go well beyond the stubbornness of your limits.

~~~

When you feel down on your luck, check the level of your effort.

Speaking For Myself

I am superstitious to this extent -- I believe that giving up before you begin is bad luck.

~~~

I know this -- that the odds are always against you if you never take the chance.

~~~

<><><>

Personality

A winning personality is not about getting people to like you; it's about getting people to like themselves when they're with you.

Observations

You don't take over a room by making everyone in it feel small. You take over a room by making everyone in it feel noticed.

~~~

People judge you by first impression. The better your first impression of them, the better they judge you.

~~~

Charisma, personality -- there are lots of labels for the knack of giving people your full attention.

~~~

<>< ><>

Pets

Keynote Thought

It is a special friend who dispels your loneliness but leaves your solitude intact.

Observations

A friend we allow into our company. A pet we allow into our solitude.

~~~

A pet is so often the answer -- when you're lonely and need company, or when you're tired of company and need lonely.

~~~

Our pets know that they are loved less than our children, but, alas, they have no sense that their need is less.

~~~

<><><>

Dogs and Cats

I had a good day with my pets -- my dog came running to greet me, and I have a 2:30 appointment with my cat.

~~~

A cat, after being scolded, goes about its business. A dog slinks off into a corner and pretends to be doing a serious self-reappraisal.

~~~

A dog is man's best friend. A cat is man's best formal acquaintance.

~~~

If you could breed a dog to a cat, you'd have man's best accomplice.

Just Cats

My cat and I have enjoyed many a silence together, a conversation always resumed exactly where left off.

~~~

Psychologists now recognize that the need to own ten cats is really a sublimated desire to own twenty cats.

~~~

Man's Best Friend

Ever wonder where you'd end up if you took your dog for a walk and never once pulled back on the leash?

~~~

The difference between a dog and a person is that when you earn a dog's love, you get it.

~~~

There is no better actor than a dog pretending to be as sad and lonely as you are.

~~~

An old dog, even more than an old spouse, always feels like doing what you feel like doing.

~~~

The most important lesson you learn from your dog is to kick a few blades of grass over it and move on.

~~~

At some point in life, you discover that nothing is fun forever, which news you then have to break to your dog.

~~~

`<><><>`

Pets

Another thing you learn from your dog is when to go lie under the dining room table and await developments.

~~~

There is a look in a dog's eyes that says, "I would gladly be your soulmate, if I only had a soul."

~~~

Life is mostly a good reason to go for a walk with your dog.

Speaking For Myself

I am accused of favoring dogs over people when, in fact, I favor whoever comes when I whistle.

~~~

I am not your dog, but if you gave me a backrub every time you saw me, I'd run to greet you, too.

~~~

I don't suppose my dog has human feelings, but he sure lets you know when you hurt his instincts.

~~~

On the whole, I would not wish to live a dog's life, except for the times when you show up to help and are told to go lie down.

~~~

I tell something to my dog, who tells another dog, who tells another, and it can be hilarious the way it comes out.

~~~

When I think of the loyalty of pets, I picture Adam and Eve leaving paradise followed by their dog.

A Speculation

Exile a man to a desert island, allowing him only his dog, and in time his self-image will conform to his dog's opinion of him. This explains why Napoleon came back for one more shot at emperor. ·

<> <> <>

Politics

Keynote Thought

No matter what the political system, its end is always its own preservation, and its means is always you.

How True, How True

Once there were kings and queens, and we were all subjects. Now there are presidents and prime ministers, and we are all objects.

~~~

Politics is always about what to do when common sense is a non-starter.

~~~

One hears little common sense spoken in politics, due to the risk of alienating its opponents.

~~~

What you find in a democracy is that it's hard to build a house when every nail has an opinion.

~~~

No political party has a monopoly on truth, in the same way that no lynch mob has a monopoly on justice.

~~~

When a politician tells you, "We're all in this together," you can be pretty sure you weren't in it before.

~~~

The first rule in politics is, "Never explain, and do so at length."

~~~

The mark of a clever conspiracy is that the people it conspires against think they are part of it. See political party.

~~~

There is scarcely one of the Ten Commandments that if acted upon in concert would not be a plot to overthrow the government.

~~~

The first test of majority rule is its willingness to educate the minority's kids.

~~~

Politics

<u>Dry, Sly and Wry</u>

Politicians don't lie, they misspeak. And they don't steal, they mispocket.

~~~

Overheard in a Washington D.C. confessional: "Bless me, Father, for sins have been committed."

~~~

There are Seven Deadly Sins, of which, so far, only Envy and Greed have organized politically.

~~~

The hope in a two-party system is that the 2+2=3 party and the 2+2=5 party can work out a compromise.

~~~

Washington D.C. classified: "Unaffiliated hack seeks party."

~~~

You can fool some of the people all of the time, also known as a base constituency.

~~~

It is a persistent delusion that electing someone to political office will get them to go away.

~~~

As between God, country and apple pie, politicians have done the least harm in the name of apple pie.

Speaking For Myself

Wouldn't it be great if voting for someone didn't have to be an act of forgiveness?

~~~

A question I always ask myself before voting is, "Would I ever want to find myself at this person's mercy?"

If You Want My Advice

Beware a politician who refers to 2 + 2 = 4 as one school of thought.

~~~

Never suppose in politics that you have heard the whole truth. Indeed, never suppose that you have heard the whole lie.

~~~

<>
<>
<>

Possessions

Keynote Thought

What a treasure are the things we have learned to live without, for no thief can take them from us.

Observations

Anything we possess that is not necessary for life or happiness becomes a burden, and not a day goes by that we don't add to it.

~~~

We realize we can't have everything, and so begins the mad dash to have everything else.

~~~

The best things in life are not only free, they require less assembly.

~~~

The thing about material possessions is that they foster a greatly exaggerated idea of what there is to lose.

~~~

The one true measure of the things that matter in life is that they can't be insured against loss.

~~~

One thing you notice early on is that there are more lines formed than things worth waiting for.

Speaking For Myself

There are things I have wanted so long that I would only consent to have them if I could keep wanting them.

~~~

I am never five minutes into stripping the clutter from my life before I start running into the clutter that is my life.

~~~

I'm not sure that people with lots of possessions are happier than the rest of us but they sure put on better yard sales.

~~~

Whew, what a dream! I dreamed a burglar broke in and left stuff.

~~~

<><><>

Possibility

Keynote Thought

*Nature decrees that we do not exceed the speed of light.
All other impossibilities are optional.*

Observations

*When it seems that something can't be done, start it, and
see if the rest of it can be done.*

~~~

*"It's impossible" is the perception. "It's never been done"
is the fact. "It's never been impossible" is the discovery.*

~~~

*The lesson of history is that everything is impossible
until some enterprising soul thinks it would be really
cool if it weren't.*

~~~

*As important as keeping a grasp on reality is keeping a
grasp on possibility.*

~~~

<>< ><>

Progress

Keynote Thought

Making a different mistake every day is not only acceptable, it is the definition of progress.

Observations

You start making progress in life when you realize that you don't always have to resume where you left off.

~~~

Progress is better measured in results that in the securement of additional funding.

~~~

When you are going around in circles, it is not progress to report a sharp increase in circles completed.

~~~

Change doesn't happen overnight; it happens when it's ready to happen -- and then it happens overnight.

~~~

<><><>

Quality in Life

There is no bridge to excellence. It is a tightrope you walk over a sheer and sudden drop into the ordinary.

Observations

The problem with settling for "good enough" is that it's so hard to distinguish it from "almost good enough."

~~~

If you don't recognize quality when you encounter it, your life tends to shape itself so that you never encounter it.

~~~

Where you find quality, you will find a craftsman, not a quality control expert.

~~~

It is easier to be good at something than to be good at faking it.

~~~

Most of the excellence we see in the world is the product not of talent or genius but of self-respect.

~~~

You only get one life, so perhaps it is worth the effort to make it your signature life.

Speaking For Myself

I would rather know that my best was not good enough than to wonder if it might have been .

The Slippery Slope

Let not the perfect be the enemy of the good.

Let not the good be the enemy of the mediocre.

Let not the mediocre be the enemy of the perfectly dreadful.

And down the slippery slope we go.

~~~

Reality

Keynote Thought

Question reality, especially if it contradicts the evidence of your hopes and dreams.

Observations

One may accept reality without necessarily accepting the current arrangement.

~~~

There is a difference between denying reality and avoiding it whenever possible.

~~~

Some, fearing reality, retreat into their imagination, but most, fearing their imagination, retreat into reality.

~~~

In the realist you have the sorry sight of the five senses deprived of their imagination.

~~~

Perception is a clash of mind and eye, the eye believing what it sees, the mind seeing what it believes.

~ ~ ~

The realist sees reality as concrete. The optimist sees reality as clay.

~ ~ ~

The hardest thing about reality is returning to it after an hour inside your child's mind.

~ ~ ~

It is said that all is illusion, but as long as there's an illusion that the kids need to be fed, all might as well be reality.

~ ~ ~

There is a time in life when the quest becomes the reality and going home again the impossible dream.

~ ~ ~

One thing you learn over the years is that the eyes can construct a figment as easily as the imagination.

~ ~ ~

Reality

Speaking For Myself

I don't deny reality, but I don't exactly go looking for it, either.

~~~

Seems like nothing brings me back to reality that makes me want to stay there.

~~~

I may accept reality, but that does not imply endorsement.

~~~

If I believe in God, it's because I have seen reality, and it's impossible to believe it is non-negotiable.

~~~

*If the world existed
But in my invention,
Wouldn't it pay me
More attention?*

~~~

<><><>

Reconciliation

Keynote Thought

There are times when two people need to step apart from one another, but there is no rule that says they have to turn and fire.

Observations

Sometimes you must take the single step that starts the journey to discover it is a journey of a single step.

~~~

It is a shame to separate from the right companion because you are on the wrong journey.

~~~

Sometimes two people need to return to an old fork in the road and, together, take the other path.

~~~

So often our greatest triumph is a willing surrender.

~~~

Reconciliation

The best solution seldom requires that one person be right and another person be wrong.

~~~

You can call it betrayal, or you can recognize that true love makes impossible promises.

~~~

*Sometimes two people
need to step apart
and make a space between
that each might see the other anew,
in a glance across a room
or silhouetted against the moon.*

~~~

Perhaps, in the end, a couple stays together for the sake of the kids -- two kids who sat under a full moon and pledged to be forever true.

~~~

<><><>

Regret

If only regret had action's purpose. If only action had regret's information.

Observations

Sometimes you can head off a decision you'll regret by looking into your heart and finding regret already there.

~~~

There are times you say things you regret because they need to be said -- and regretted.

~~~

One way to stop doing things you'll later regret is to stop doing things you already regret.

~~~

Worse than regretting on Tuesday what you failed to do on Monday is realizing on Wednesday that it was not too late on Tuesday.

~~~

<>‹›‹›

Relationships

Keynote Thought

There are times in a relationship when the band plays,
but mostly you dance to a remembered tune.

Observations

No matter how passionate the relationship, it is
sustained in the end by its everyday courtesies.

~~~

The way to make a relationship better is to appreciate it
just the way it is.

~~~

The saddest thing in a relationship is trying to make it
last by never letting it begin.

~~~

Whether a relationship begins by Fate or Chance, it
nearly always endures by Second Chance.

~~~

A truce is not a relationship, and if you are the only one observing it, it's not a truce, either.

~~~

In every relationship there are situations you need to talk through -- and situations where you need to be through talking.

~~~

No relationship is as strong as it can be until it has survived the thing most likely to destroy it.

~~~

The best relationship is the one that makes you feel good about the person at your end of it.

~~~

Even the best of relationships end -- a reason to always keep on hand a bottle of champagne and two glasses.

~~~

We all know the part of ourselves that needs to be harnessed. It takes someone else to know the part that needs to be set free.

~~~

The Intimate Bond

A loving relationship can become fun, but it's more likely that a fun relationship will become love.

~~~

Once you find someone to share your ups and downs, downs are almost as good as ups.

~~~

To truly know someone is to know the silence that stands for the thing they never speak of.

~~~

As important as shared memories is the silent agreement that certain things never happened.

~~~

There comes a time in a relationship when you realize that you love someone enough to let them keep their secrets.

~~~

There are moments when two people need to put on the brave face they show to the world and show it to each other.

~~~

We are, many of us, a planet orbiting somebody's sun, unconscious of a lonely moon, orbiting our planet.

~~~

To stay in a relationship rather than hurt your partner may not be love, but it usually seems that way to an outside observer.

~~~

Sometimes a lasting relationship just comes down to two people wanting it to be the way it was.

If You Want My Advice

Never leave a relationship while it's still important to you that the other person understand why.

~~~

The Voice of Experience

In the perfect partnership, one dreams dreams and the other dreams financing.

~~~

<><><>

Responsibility

Keynote Thought

At some point you must decide if you want to succeed or just be someone who was never to blame for anything going wrong.

Observations

Never hesitate to take the blame, for it puts the blame where you can do something about it.

~~~

When there is hell to pay, it is usually cheaper to pay it than to finance an endless purgatory.

~~~

As a rule of thumb, the higher your position of responsibility, the less likely you will ever have to take responsibility for anything.

~~~

<><><>

Sanity

Keynote Thought

*To be sane is to know that there are parts of the mind
you cannot enter with any hope of returning.*

Observations

*Madness is defined in different ways at different times,
sanity being the ability to keep current.*

~~~

*There is no sane person who does not at times deny
reality in order to stay sane.*

~~~

*We are all multiple personalities, the sane among us
having the knack of settling on one spokesperson.*

~~~

<><><>

Sanity

Among creatures born into chaos, some will imagine an order, others will passively accept the order, and the rest will be pronounced insane.

Dry, Sly and Wry

The problem with a severe delusional state is that it attracts followers.

~~~

The paranoid believes that sinister forces are out to get him, not realizing that they are out to get everybody.

~~~

Insanity is doing the same thing over and over again, expecting a raise.

~~~

One thing I know is that I'm never going to plead temporary insanity, there being so little evidence that it's temporary.

~~~

<><><>

Self-Esteem

Keynote Thought

Oh, what we might accomplish if it weren't for an exaggerated sense of our own unimportance.

Observations

Lend, by your imperfections, self-esteem to others, and you will be invited everywhere.

~~~

Be thoughtful of others, and you will not be shy, for they are incompatible addictions.

~~~

If we could see others as they see themselves, our shyness would soon become compassion.

~~~

<><><>

Self-Interest

Keynote Thought

You do not wake up one morning a bad person. It happens by a thousand tiny surrenders of self-respect to self-interest.

Observations

What you must realize about self-interest is that it loves to pose as your better judgment.

~~~

The thing about selfish motives is that you can mistake them for principles and send your kids to die for them.

~~~

One's conscience should never be apprised of one's property holdings.

~~~

<><><>

Siblings

Keynote Thought

There is a bond forged between two people who have hid together under the same bed.

Observations

The advantage of growing up with siblings is that you become very good at fractions.

~~~

There is a strong chance that siblings who turn out well were hassled by the same parents.

~~~

A toast once heard: "To my big sister, who never found her second Easter egg until I'd found my first."

~~~

Social Networking

Keynote Thought

The great thing about social networking is that you get to meet people you would otherwise meet only if you were in the same therapy group.

Observations

A social networker is a normal person who happens to have a need to count his or her friends every half hour.

~~~

Trouble is, if you're not into social networking, people think you're anti-social when you're only anti-networking.

~~~

One thing social networking has made possible is the application of mob psychology without having to assemble a mob.

~~~

<><><>

Solitude

Keynote Thought

I enjoy both company and solitude, and in the company of my solitude, I find both.

Observations

There are times when you seek your solitude, and your solitude just wants to be left alone.

~~~

What a blessing to be alone with your thoughts when so many are alone with their inability to think.

~~~

No matter how reclusive we tend to be, we picture the afterlife as a community of souls. It is one thing to seek privacy in this life; it is another to face eternity alone.

~~~

Two's company, three's a crowd, which leaves us to discover for ourselves what <u>one</u> is.

~~~

<><><>

Solitude

There is a part of us that stands in silent witness to what we do, waiting for a solitary moment to bring up the subject.

~~~

Speaking For Myself

I have always needed a place to go to as refuge from the crowd -- and a crowd to go to as refuge from that place.

~~~

There are times when I'm alone with my thoughts, which is to say, not alone enough.

~~~

Forsaking my friends, I sought my solitude, only to discover that my solitude preferred my friends.

~~~

You can wander a loneliness alone, but it takes two to explore a solitude.

~~~

<><><>

Soulmates

Keynote Thought

*There doesn't have to be anyone who understands you.
There just has to be someone who wants to.*

Observations

*In the end you don't so much find yourself as you find
someone who knows who you are.*

~~~

*One day, in your search for happiness, you find a
partner by your side, and you realize that your
happiness has come to help you search.*

~~~

*Eventually soulmates meet, for they have the same
hiding place.*

~~~

<><><>

Soulmates

*You will not find a soulmate in the quiet of your room.
You must go to a noisy place and look in the quiet
corners.*

~~~

*What we find in a soulmate is not something wild to
tame but something wild to run with.*

~~~

*In a soulmate we find not company but a completed
solitude.*

~~~

*Eventually, if you're lucky in life, you find someone with
the same chemical imbalance you have.*

~~~

*Sometimes it is worth getting lost to see who will come
looking for us.*

~~~

*When something is missing in our lives, it usually turns
out to be someone.*

~~~

<>‹›‹>

Soulmates

To find someone who will love you for no reason, and to shower that person with reasons, that is the ultimate happiness.

~~~

Having perfected our disguise, we spend our lives searching for someone we don't fool.

~~~

You list all the reasons why no one could ever love you, and then one day you find someone with the same list.

~~~

There are few greater joys than having a dream you cannot let go of and a partner who would never ask you to.

~~~

There is no motivation like a world that thinks you can't and a partner who thinks you can.

~~~

Sometimes two people meet who have no illusions and discover they are ready for one.

~~~

229

<><><>

Soulmates

*A soulmate is someone who knows where you went
when you were last seen wandering aimlessly.*

~~~

*You can be happy with someone who likes you despite
your faults -- until you meet someone who likes your
faults.*

~~~

*There is never just one loose end, so if you're feeling like
a loose end, you can be sure someone else is, too.*

~~~

*To truly know someone is to know the silence that
stands for the thing they never speak of.*

Dry, Sly and Wry

*When two people like the same music and the same
movies, they can usually work out differences in politics
and religion.*

~~~

Speaking For Myself

Sometimes, I believe, we are allowed to get lost that we might find the right person to ask directions of.

~~~

Born to loving parents and grandparents, we grow up thinking the world is full of people who will place our happiness above their own. We find, if we are lucky in life, that there is exactly one more.

~~~

To find a loving partner is to win the only first place prize that matters in life -- and it's seldom even a competition.

Lines From Unfinished Novels

"She was a walker in the rain, a stroller in the sand, a frequenter of places where nobody goes -- and they kept meeting."

~~~

*"He was a sad and lonesome clown,
And she was the circus that came to town."*

~~~

<>·<>·<>

Success

Keynote Thought

The trick to succeeding is to stop thinking there's a trick to everything.

Observations

Success is a tale of obstacles overcome, and for every obstacle overcome, an excuse not used.

~~~

You know you're succeeding when the people telling you it can't be done start changing their reasons.

~~~

The first requirement of success is to show up. The second is to make it clear you're not leaving.

~~~

The road to success is not a path you find but a trail you blaze.

~~~

Try to discover
The road to success,
And you'll seek but never find;
But blaze your own path,
And the road to success
Will trail right behind.

~~~

You embark on the road to success when you stop dreaming dreams and start dreaming plans.

~~~

Every partial failure is a partial success, so if you haven't succeeded, maybe you haven't had enough partial failures.

~~~

So often we are kept from our goal not by obstacles but by a clear path to a lesser goal.

~~~

One key to success is to have lunch at the time of day most people have breakfast.

~~~

<><><>

Success

You can write a success story or a hard-luck story out of the same set of excuses.

~~~

What makes the road to success so difficult is that beyond the phony excuses lie the perfectly good ones.

~~~

Many a successful person would have settled for less, but no one ever offered them less.

~~~

What you discover about people who have all that life offers is that they didn't wait for it to be offered.

~~~

It's always good to admit when you've failed, by way of establishing who gets to decide.

If You Want My Advice

Do not envy another person's success unless you can recall envying their struggle.

~~~

We all make mistakes. The trick is to make your mistakes big enough so that they don't seem like only one person's fault.

~~~

Remember this -- that you and you alone are the absolute and final judge of whether you are a success.

~~~

The Voice of Experience

The surest sign that the goal is near
Is that offers of help begin to appear.

And One For The Road

In the end it's pretty simple -- the road to success is wherever people need another road.

~~~

<> <> <>

Time

Keynote Thought

No matter how you rush about, you will notice at the end of the day that you traveled at the speed of time.

Observations

Another day, another chance to travel into tomorrow's past and change it.

~~~

We are all time-sharers on planet Earth. We are not asked to leave it a better place. We are merely asked not to break the furniture or stain the rug.

~~~

Time is a figure eight, at its center the city of Deja Vu.

~~~

There are three dimensions of time, two containing better days.

~~~

*First God created time. Then God created man that
man might, in the course of time, perfect himself. Then
God decided He'd better create eternity.*

~~~

*One day in your busy life, there's a knock at the door,
and a voice says, "Come, I will show you where the
time went."*

~~~

*Nothing lasts forever, although we often underestimate
how long it will last in the meantime.*

~~~

*The miracle of the loaves and fishes is nothing
compared to the miracle of the 24 hours, which the
Lord distributes among the multitude such that each
gets the whole 24.*

~~~

*Time brings an end to everything, often mistaken for a
tragedy.*

~~~

*For centuries, man believed that the sun revolves
around the Earth. Centuries later, he still believes that
time travels clockwise.*

~~~

<><><>

Time

It's a lesser regret to have spent time foolishly than to have let it expire unused.

Speaking For Myself

I have never wished for more hours in the day, twenty-four being more than I have time for as it is.

~~~

I suspect that time is to eternity what a waterspout is to the ocean -- a brief disturbance on its surface.

~~~

I live on a tiny planet orbiting a minor star. Every time the planet completes an orbit, I count off a segment of my life. Why do I do this? I dunno, it passes the time.

~~~

Of all the ways I can think of to achieve immortality, living forever seems the least useful to anybody.

~~~

Tolerance

Keynote Thought

I look into the faces of people struggling with their own lives, and I do not see strangers.

Observations

A good part of tolerance is just letting others live by the same deceptions we allow ourselves.

~~~

I have never understood the purpose of hate, or how you know the purpose has been accomplished and you can stop.

~~~

An important corollary to the Golden Rule is to leave others be as you would have them leave you be.

~~~

I do not object to any life style, unless you insist I adopt it, nor any religion, unless you insist I practice it.

~~~

<><><>

Truth & Lies

<u>Keynote Thought</u>

If there be no God, then what is truth but the average of all lies.

<u>Observations</u>

To deny any truth is to begin a chain of denial that must eventually deny every truth there is.

~~~

Worse than telling a lie is spending the rest of your life staying true to a lie.

~~~

It is tolerable -- the lie that gets you through your days, if you can return to a truth that gets you through your nights.

~~~

A clever liar always underestimates the cleverness of the truth.

~~~

The first step toward telling the truth is to tell the whole lie.

~~~

Every lie is two lies -- the lie we tell others and the lie we tell ourselves to justify it.

~~~

Sometimes it isn't a lie; it is just the truth broken very gently.

~~~

Somewhere between the honest truth and the deceptive lie is the deceptive truth and the honest lie.

~~~

It is possible to know the truth about someone and not be the person they need to hear it from.

~~~

Every lie has a reason, the reason also a lie.

~~~

One of life's simpler rules: Never put yourself in the position of being harmed by someone telling the truth.

~~~

<><><>

War

Keynote Thought

There is no excuse for war so cynical that it won't seem noble after the first soldier has died for it.

Observations

The problem with a country defending its honor is that it always defends more honor than it has.

~~~

Man, in his sensitivity, does not give names to animals he intends to slaughter but goes on giving names to children he intends to send to war.

~~~

You can lose the battle and win the war. You can even lose the war and win the post-war.

~~~

The only lesson any general ever learned from war is not to invade Russia in summer uniform.

~~~

<><><>

Wealth

Keynote Thought

Wealth and wisdom are seldom combined, for the person who achieves one no longer desires the other.

Observations

Measure wealth not by the money you have but by the things you have for which you would not take money.

~~~

The problem with spending your life seeking wealth is that you never get wealthy enough to buy back your life.

~~~

Material success is always tempered by the recollection that there was some sort of happiness that was supposed to come with it.

~~~

The basic dilemma of politics is that there is less wealth than there are fair shares.

~~~

<>< ><>

Wealth

Youthful idealism is the belief that the portion of our parents' wealth not being used to put us through college should be distributed among the needy of the world.

~~~

It is an assumption of the rich that those who are happy with little will be happier with less.

~~~

It is not the wealthy who shape the world but they who have no price.

Dry, Sly and Wry

It doesn't seem fair that a greedy few should have all the wealth when the rest of us are just as greedy.

~~~

Money always ends up in the hands of the rich, first going through a money-laundering operation called the economy.

~~~

Everyone favors the redistribution of wealth, the wealthy favoring the way it's already been redistributed.

~~~

<>◇<>

Women

Keynote Thought

As long as there are women in the world, men will have a greatly exaggerated idea of how many things take care of themselves.

Observations

A man finds love and is satisfied. A woman finds love and insists on turning it into happiness.

~~~

A man sometimes wins an argument, but a woman always wins a silence.

~~~

Only a man is allowed to give up. There is always someone for whom a woman must carry on.

~~~

Women

One of the great logical puzzles is how every woman is just like her mother but nothing like her sister.

~~~

Sometimes a woman marries a man for what he has, and sometimes she marries a man because she is all he has.

~~~

The first job of motherhood is to get a child to the point where its father is ready for fatherhood.

~~~

There is no bond between men like the bond forged between two women who have shared a good cry.

~~~

There is an instinct in a woman to love most her own child -- and an instinct to make any child who needs her love, her own.

~~~

Writing

The first goal of writing is to have one's words read successfully.

Observations

If it doesn't work horizontally as prose,
it
probably
won't
work
any
better
vertically
pretending
to be
poetry.

~~~

The aphorist sees in every truth a wise saying, and in every contradiction, two wise sayings.

~~~

You Are Probably A Writer

Are you an artist? Look about you. Is there some
physical tool -- brush, chisel, musical instrument --
whose use you have mastered? Is there a part of your
body -- voice, hands, feet -- that responds utterly to
your command? If so, you are an artist. If not, you
are probably a writer.

~~~

<><><>

~~~

Afterthoughts

~~~

Afterthoughts

If you can't explain it in a few words, try fewer.

~~~

There is a logical explanation for everything, often mistaken for the reason it happened.

~~~

Why worry -- it's not the end of the world. And if it is, why worry?

~~~

People are resilient. After all, every person born has recovered from nine months on life support.

~~~

I have never heard the words, "There is no easy way to tell you this," without thinking afterwards that there was an easier way.

~~~

I have never met anyone who wanted to save the world without my financial support.

~~~

It is hard to resist a flatterer who gets it right.

~~~

*One is more apt to become wise by doing fool things
than by reading wise sayings.*

~~~

*Massage is the only form of physical pleasure to which
nature forgot to attach consequences.*

~~~

*Well, it finally happened -- a lawsuit for wrongful
doing unto others as you would have them do unto you.*

~~~

*One way to know you were meant for a higher calling
is that you can't get hired for any of the lower ones.*

~~~

*IRS: an agency modeled after the revenue-raising
concepts of the 19th-century economist, Jesse James.*

~~~

*Words from the past: "It's a clever idea, Mr. Bell, but
don't wire us, we'll wire you."*

~~~

The explanation is always longer when there isn't any.

~~~

<><><>

Afterthoughts

Nowadays you envy a manic-depressive. Half the time he's happy, the other half he's right.

~~~

As to the Seven Deadly Sins, I deplore pride, wrath, lust, envy and greed. Gluttony and sloth I pretty much plan my day around.

~~~

You can spend too much time wondering which of identical twins is the more alike.

~~~

How do you know when enough is enough? Hint: enough is always enough.

~~~

Inscribed on a cave dweller's wall: "They who do not know history are condemned to start it."

~~~

Always telling the truth is no doubt better than always lying but equally pathological.

~~~

<><><>

Afterthoughts

I look at it this way -- I'm not an eavesdropper; I have an attention-surplus disorder.

~~~

Less is owed to courage than to the mistaken belief that there is nothing to be afraid of.

~~~

Overheard at a wake: "Thank God she didn't live to see what the mortician did with her hair."

~~~

People say to you, "What good will worrying do?", as if you were worrying for the good it will do.

~~~

I believe there is a little good in everyone, although if there isn't, that would pretty much explain everything.

~~~

And God said, "Be fruitful and multiply," whereupon he created the moon, saying, "Let there be indirect lighting."

~~~

<><><>

Afterthoughts

Most people would rather defend to the death your right to say it than listen to it.

~~~

There's a whole list of scams I might fall for -- if I knew how to wire money to Nigeria.

~~~

One thing all religions agree on is that after six days of breakfast, lunch and dinner, there should be one day of brunch and supper.

~~~

Sign over the gates of hell: "Doesn't mean you're a bad person."

~~~

Sign over the gates of hell: "Immediate delivery anywhere in the world."

~~~

The object of most prayers is to wangle an advance on good intentions.

~~~

<><><>

I dunno, you get to an age when no recent photo of yourself seems recent enough.

~~~

Ever wonder what crime you committed that you're confined to a small enclosure above your sinuses under permanent skull arrest?

~~~

My health plan doesn't cover dental, so I enrolled my teeth as 32 dependents, each needing a complete physical once a year.

~~~

The trouble with having a physical body is that people know it's where you hang out, and you don't get any privacy.

~~~

It never fails. Whenever I'm asked to name the Seven Wharfs, I always forget Dock.

~~~

Classified ad: "Bundle of good intentions seeks mindreader."

~~~

<><><>

Afterthoughts

A simple rule -- never let anything that doesn't matter to you ruin something that does.

~~~

The only thing known for certain about the next life is that you get there ahead of your luggage.

~~~

You don't realize how inaccurate network TV reporting is until they do a story in your hometown.

~~~

The hardest thing about reshaping minds is getting to them before the cement dries.

~~~

Perhaps God gives us a physical body so that every time we change our mind, we won't be someone else.

~~~

The way to play second fiddle is to play it like second Stradivarius.

~~~

Bumper sticker: "I brake for flashing blue lights."

~~~

Do I rue a life wasted doing crosswords? Yes, but I do know the three-letter word for regret.

~~~

You learn by doing, and what you usually learn is not to do it again.

~~~

Despite the goings-on in Congress, I don't believe the U.S. is bordering on madness. I think Canada and Mexico are.

~~~

I dunno, you get to a point in life when you'd settle for life, liberty and the pursuit of "can't complain."

~~~

Stored away in some brain cell is the image of a long-departed aunt that you haven't thought of in thirty years. Stored away in another cell is the image of a pink pony stitched on your first set of baby pajamas. All it takes to get that aunt mounted on the back of that pony is to eat a slab of meatloaf immediately before going to bed.

~~~

Made in the USA
Monee, IL
28 July 2022

10474631R00152